T0302075

Cambridge Elements ≡

Elements in Development Economics
Series Editor-in-Chief
Kunal Sen
UNU-WIDER and University of Manchester

CHILEAN ECONOMIC DEVELOPMENT UNDER NEOLIBERALISM

Structural Transformation, High Inequality and Environmental Fragility

Andrés Solimano
International Center for Globalization and Development

Gabriela Zapata-Román
Universidad Central de Chile

Shaftesbury Road, Cambridge CB2 8EA, United Kingdom

One Liberty Plaza, 20th Floor, New York, NY 10006, USA

477 Williamstown Road, Port Melbourne, VIC 3207, Australia

314–321, 3rd Floor, Plot 3, Splendor Forum, Jasola District Centre,
New Delhi – 110025, India

103 Penang Road, #05–06/07, Visioncrest Commercial, Singapore 238467

Cambridge University Press is part of Cambridge University Press & Assessment,
a department of the University of Cambridge.

We share the University's mission to contribute to society through the pursuit of
education, learning and research at the highest international levels of excellence.

www.cambridge.org
Information on this title: www.cambridge.org/9781009477345

DOI: 10.1017/9781009477352

First published 2024

A catalogue record for this publication is available from the British Library

ISBN 978-1-009-47734-5 Hardback
ISBN 978-1-009-47738-3 Paperback
ISSN 2755-1601 (online)
ISSN 2755-1598 (print)

Chilean Economic Development under Neoliberalism

Structural Transformation, High Inequality and Environmental Fragility

Elements in Development Economics

DOI: 10.1017/9781009477352
First published online: January 2024

Andrés Solimano
International Center for Globalization and Development

Gabriela Zapata-Román
Universidad Central de Chile

Author for correspondence: Andrés Solimano, asolimano@ciglob.org

Abstract: This Element examines Chile's economic development over the past fifty years or so under the neoliberal model in terms of its impacts on growth, inflation, income and wealth distribution, and structural change. The analysis includes a historical perspective from the nineteenth century to the present and combines economic analysis with a political economy approach. This title is also available as Open Access on Cambridge Core.

Keywords: Chile, economic development, growth and inflation, social inequality, democracy

ISBNs: 9781009477345 (HB), 9781009477383 (PB), 9781009477352 (OC)
ISSNs: 2755-1601 (online), 2755-1598 (print)

Contents

1 Introduction

The purpose of this Element is to examine the economic, social, and development policies applied in Chile and their outcomes in the past six decades with an emphasis on the long cycle of the neoliberal model built around market deregulation, privatization, and a minimal state. This model started to be applied, under authoritarian conditions, in the mid-1970s, and it has continued with democratic governments – although with some regulations – since the 1990s. The Element looks at the patterns of structural change and macroeconomic and growth policies since around the 1960s, describing the often-complex process of stabilizing inflation and adjusting to macroeconomic imbalances. We also stress throughout the Element the social consequences of the neoliberal model, particularly its record of high inequality. The importance of political economy and historical conditions in shaping Chilean development is also emphasized.

The Chilean case is important from a global perspective as Chile was a sort of pioneer in the implementation of neoliberal economic policies in the 1970s when these policies were not tried in other countries, although they became more popular in the 1980s, 1990s, and thereafter with the demise of the Soviet Bloc and the preeminence of the Washington Consensus. The Chilean economic model has been portrayed as a success story when presented in terms of growth acceleration, macroeconomic stability, and export-led growth, but this rosy assessment tends to neglect important issues of deindustrialization, financialization, ecological deterioration, and persistent inequality that have accompanied its implementation. This Element seeks to carry out a more balanced assessment of the Chilean development experience.

Chile is a small country of nearly 20 million people located at the southernmost part of South America, rich in mineral resources, with long coastal areas and good agricultural lands. Its human resources base is reasonably well educated and poverty has declined, but it is still a socially stratified country with indices of high income and wealth inequality.

The economic structure of the country changed in various ways following policies of trade liberalization and privatization of state-owned enterprises such as telecommunications and utilities undertaken in the 1970s and 1980s under General Augusto Pinochet's regime. These policies included reducing tariffs, deregulating goods, labor, and capital markets, and promoting foreign investment. Much emphasis has been placed on the increase in per capita incomes since the 1990s, which is true, but growth has been accompanied by a strong reliance on natural resources along with deindustrialization – that is, a steady reduction in the share of manufacturing in gross domestic product (GDP) from nearly 25 percent in 1972 (peak) to 10 percent in 2018. In addition, the services sector expanded sharply with a rise in the importance of the financial sector and the growth of commerce and nonessential services. In turn, the economy became very specialized in the exports of raw copper and, later, of lithium with a low level of processing in line with an extractive model. Fresh fruits, wine, timber, salmon, and other sea products are also part of the Chilean export basket.

Historically, the country has relied for its development on nitrate, copper, coal, and gold, along with agricultural products such as wheat. Two long cycles of commodity dependence can be distinguished: a nitrate cycle (mainly exploited by British companies and financed by British banks) from around 1880 to the early 1930s, and a copper cycle (dominated by US companies) that started in the 1930s when copper replaced nitrate as the main export commodity, mainly directed to the American market. In the early 1970s, sizeable foreign copper corporations were nationalized. Nowadays, the share of copper in total exports remains close to 50 percent, but its contribution to fiscal revenues has diminished (see Section 2).

Early in the twentieth century (ca. 1900–20), nitrate exports accounted for 65–80 percent of total exports and nearly 40 percent of GDP.[1] Moreover, nitrate taxes funded almost 50 percent of total public expenditure. In the late 1920s and early 1930s, the boom in Chilean natural nitrates ended after Germany developed synthetic nitrate at a lower cost. Chilean nitrate production declined by nearly 75 percent between 1928 and 1934, prompting a severe economic and social crisis in the country (output decline, high unemployment, and poverty) that was exacerbated by the Great Depression.[2]

The Great Depression that originated in core economies hit the Chilean economy very hard. After a complex recovery starting about 1933–4, the country switched in the early 1940s from a commodity-export-oriented growth pattern to an import-substitution industrialization (ISI) strategy that aimed to reduce external economic dependence. New industries in the energy, iron and steel, sugar, and telecommunications sectors were created by a publicly owned development corporation, the Corporación de Fomento de la Producción (CORFO), as part of the industrialization effort.[3]

The period of ISI that helped build an industrial base of state-owned and private-sector companies was accompanied by growing urbanization and the expansion of education, healthcare services, and social security in the context of uninterrupted democratic rule. Nonetheless, this period also coincided with an acceleration of inflation in Chile, particularly in the 1950s, 1960s, and 1970s, when inflation reached three-digit levels. A combination of fiscal imbalances

---

[1] Sunkel and Cariola (1982).   [2] Lüders and colleagues (2016).   [3] Solimano (2020).

occurred, partly financed by money creation (loans from the central bank to the treasury), along with distributive conflict between labor – growing more powerful through nation-based labor unions – and capital. The conflict over income shares between workers and capital owners was reflected in wage demands after price increases to protect the purchasing power of wages and adjustment of markups by firms to protect profit shares. Inflationary pressures also came from recurrent currency devaluations and imported inflation.

The ISI policy, standard in most Latin American countries, increased local productive development, but it could not isolate the country entirely from the effects of external shocks and dependence on foreign capital. The small size of Chile's domestic market – unlike those of Brazil, Argentina, and Mexico – did not allow for the effective development of capital-intensive industries such as the automotive and heavy machinery industries (Ffrench-Davis, 1973). Despite this, by the end of the 1950s, the manufacturing industry represented around 21 percent of the Chilean economy.

In 1950–70, the share of exports in GDP declined substantially and fluctuated between 7 and 9 percent. Copper incomes in that period represented 55–65 percent of total exports and 15–30 percent of total fiscal revenues. Copper mine ownership was a contentious issue as Chile tried to recover the copper sector for the state. In the 1960s, copper mines were "Chileanized" under a scheme of mixed property ownership between the Chilean state and American companies. In 1971, under Salvador Allende's government, copper mines were fully nationalized with the support of all political parties from both the left wing, center and right wing. After the military coup of September 1973, although copper nationalization was not legally reversed, the copper sector experienced de facto privatization through policies that encouraged faster growth in private copper mining rather than the expansion of publicly owned mines, whose share in total copper production steadily declined in the decades thereafter.

The bloody military coup that deposed the Allende government in 1973 marked the end of Chilean democracy for seventeen years as the parliament was closed, political parties were declared in recess or banned, labor union activity was curtailed, and no free press was permitted. The military junta developed an active repression against political and social dissent, resulting in thousands of killings, disappearances, torture, and exile. In the economic sphere, the military regime applied shock treatment in the fiscal and monetary areas to reduce the rate of price increases, but inflation proved sticky. The military, along with a group of Chilean economists trained in Chicago, deregulated markets, privatized a score of state-owned enterprises, curbed labor unions, and cut import tariffs and restrictions to the mobility of international capital. A severe economic and financial crisis developed between 1981 and 1983, but the economy slowly recovered toward the second half of the 1980s amid extended social protests, particularly in 1983 and 1984, for the reduction of unemployment, more economic security, and the restoration of democracy.

In the early 1990s, after free elections, democracy was restored, but this came with strings attached: Pinochet's economic model could not be abandoned, the constitution of 1980 approved under military rule was to be preserved, the military junta could not be prosecuted for massive human rights violations, and labor unions had to remain weak and marginalized. It was a controlled democracy in which primacy was given to the maintenance of the neoliberal economic framework and the influence of the military and big economic conglomerates.

Aggregate economic growth rose rapidly from the mid-to-late 1980s to around 1998, and then it started to slow down, mostly in the period 2010–20. Particularly noticeable is the trend for slower productivity growth from around 2005–6 to the present, suggesting the lack of dynamism of a growth model based on extractive industry, financialization of the economy, and exports of semi-processed forestry products, fish, and water-intensive fruits. A rent-based economy may not be sustainable in the long run. If evaluated by the criteria of the United Nations Sustainable Development Goals (UNSDGs) for 2030, stressing social equity, ecological sustainability, participatory development, productive diversification, and other socioeconomic goals, Chilean development is in need of substantive redirection.

From the mid-1990s to 2020, inflationary pressures receded because of lower prices in manufacturing goods imported mainly from China, the moderation of wage demands by weak labor unions, and the policies of an independent central bank with a strong anti-inflationary mandate. However, after the COVID-19 pandemic in 2022, Chile experienced a return to inflation in the 10–15 percent annual range, up from 3–4 percent in the previous two decades, although inflation started to recede in 2023. Energy and food price shocks and liquidity accumulation during the pandemic have been identified as important sources of the acceleration in inflation; on the other side, since September 2021, the Banco Central de Chile (Central Bank of Chile) has, each month for more than a year and a half, raised interest rates to cool demand and inflation.

Macroeconomic cycles have been a permanent feature of the Chilean economy. The most severe recessions in the past 100 years took place in 1930–2, 1975, and 1982–3. In all of these episodes, annual GDP declined by more than 10 percent. Then smaller recessions (GDP declining by 1–2 percent) occurred in 1999 (Asian financial crisis), 2009 (subprime crisis), and 2020, at the time of the COVID pandemic, when GDP declined by 6 percent.

1.1 Social Dimensions

The social dimensions of the neoliberal Chilean model of the past fifty years are problematic as they have been accompanied by persistent inequality. In the mid-1970s, macroeconomic shock treatment and rapid trade and financial liberalization led to significant declines in real wages, curtailment of social spending, persistently high unemployment, and a decline in the labor share in national income. These trends were aggravated in the crisis of 1982–3 but partially reversed in the mid-to-late 1980s. Since the 1990s, poverty rates have declined, quite sharply in statistical terms, although the size of these reductions is very different depending on what methodology is used and whether we refer to income poverty and multidimensional poverty, the latter including access to social services.

The combination of faster GDP growth and more generous social policies implemented after the return to democracy account for the reduction in income poverty in the 1990s and 2000s. However, when other measures of well-being are used such as consumption percentiles and multidimensional poverty (shortfalls in access to education, healthcare, housing, pensions, social support networks), the picture is less encouraging and poverty levels are much higher than traditional statistics suggest.

The social structure of Chile comprises powerful economic elites who seek to preserve the status quo in alliance with political elites. This is a historical constant. Historical studies that have computed income Gini coefficients from around 1850 to 2010 show that the index has moved, persistently, in the range of 50–60 percent for the whole period, showing the persistence of high inequality over more than a century and a half. This range of inequality is very high by international standards. Only from 2006 has the Gini coefficient dropped to less than 50 percent, reaching 44 percent in 2017. Chile appears as the second most unequal country among the Organisation for Economic Co-operation and Development (OECD) countries (OECD, 2018a) and among the top ten to fifteen most unequal countries in the world.[4] In turn, the richest 1 percent of the population captures nearly one-third of national income.[5]

The inequality of personal wealth (financial and nonfinancial assets) is much higher than the inequality of income flow. Gini coefficients for personal wealth calculated for Chile by the World International Database (WID) of the Paris School of Economics are close to 90 percent, although other sources put the index closer to 70 percent. Worldwide wealth inequality is substantially higher than the inequality of income flow, and Chile is no exception. Policies of privatization, booms in asset prices held by a minority of high-net-worth

---

[4] Solimano (2016).   [5] López and colleagues (2013).

individuals, and higher savings rates for upper-income groups are all factors contributing to high wealth inequality.

Historically, a main feature of Chilean inequality has been inequality in landownership. The political economy of development has evolved over time, but a constant feature is the high political influence of powerful economic proprietary elites. In the nineteenth century, after independence, effective power shifted from a Spanish-born elite to a Chilean-born elite of landowners, mine owners, merchants, industrialists, and financiers. However, the overall income and wealth gaps between elites and the rest of the population remained after independence in the republican period. Currently, a skewed distribution of the holding of financial assets and productive wealth (mining, industry, banking) is a main source of wealth inequality in the country. In turn, income inequality is accompanied by generally modest wage levels due to the weak bargaining power of labor and skills shortages, unequal access to education, and lack of upward social mobility in a socially stratified society. Since the 1980s, public education has been consistently de-financed by the state, and this affects upward social mobility and reduces access to good economic opportunities for low-income groups and the middle class.

1.2 Organization of the Element

This Element is organized in five sections besides this introduction. Section 2 provides a historical overview of the Chilean society and economy from the nineteenth century until the present, including macroeconomic developments, changes in development strategies, main economic and political crises, and constitutional changes. Section 3 focuses on the patterns of structural transformation of the Chilean economy, reflecting sector changes in output and employment between industry, mining, agriculture, and services. Section 4 discusses inflation, growth, and inequality in Chile, addressing interactions and trade-offs along with the different objectives and policy options to deal with them. This section underscores the deindustrialization and financialization trends the Chilean economy has experienced in recent decades. Section 5 focuses on poverty, inequality, and social policy and reviews empirical evidence regarding the decline in poverty and the maintenance of high inequality in recent decades, examining measurement issues and the need to look at wealth distribution and not only income distribution as an indicator of the medium- to long-run prospectus of future inequality. The section also discusses complexity and social segmentation associated with the private-sector delivery of education, healthcare, and the private management of pension funds – key ingredients of neoliberal social policy. Section 6 provides a synthesis of the Element's main conclusions and highlights future challenges for more sustainable, balanced, and socially inclusive development in Chile.

2 Chilean Development Models, Crises, and Constitutional History: A Long-Run Perspective

2.1 Introduction

During the colonial period, Chile was a relatively small economy, mostly rural, specializing in agriculture, fishing, and mining products such as gold, silver, copper, and nitrate. It imported manufactured goods and exported mining and agricultural products. Nonetheless, gold and silver deposits were much smaller than in Mexico and Peru. Spanish colonizers were assigned land and had dominion over Indigenous workers through the modality of *encomienda*. Trade was allowed only with Spain and maritime routes were controlled by the crown, although this was partly changed during the Bourbon Reforms. The social structure was composed of three broad segments: an elite of *pensinsulares* (a ruling segment born in Spain) and *criollos* (Spanish descendants born in the colony who served as colonial administrators); a middle class of small producers, artisans, and traders called *mestizos* (people of mixed European and Indigenous descent); and a popular stratum of mulattos, peasants, Indigenous workers, and black slaves.

Chile gained independence from the Spanish crown in the early nineteenth century; however, political independence did not automatically bring economic equality and inclusive development to the country. The dominant elites, as stated in Section 1, mostly changed from foreign to local. On September 18, 1810, the *criollo* leaders of Santiago declared independence from Spain; seven years later, on February 12, 1817, Bernardo O'Higgins Riquelme, the "Father of Chile," defeated the Spanish and thereafter became Supreme Director of Chile. O'Higgins subscribed a one million sterling sovereign loan from British commercial banks to help build a Chilean navy, finance basic physical infrastructure, and kick off a new public administration run by Chileans.

Since its first strides toward independence, Chile has had ten constitutions. The first three (1811, 1812, and 1814) were attempts to legitimize Chile's independence from Spain. After the expulsion of the *realistas* (the group who supported the Spanish monarchy) and during the O'Higgins government, two more constitutions were written, in 1818 and in 1822, both with a marked nationalist spirit. Another in 1823 was written by conservative Juan Egaña but was largely a discordant initiative at a time of mounting liberalism. After Chile's first provisional constitution was approved by direct democratic vote in August 1818, conservatives and liberals engaged in a twelve-year civil war in which the country's constitution was changed four times according to which-ever group maintained power. But the fierce opposition of the conservatives, along with even stauncher resistance from the so-called *estanqueros* – politi-cians led by Diego Portales and associated with the *estanco* contract (regulating tobacco, liquor, and gambling) – led finally to their strident demand for a strong government and an end to social disorder.

After a failed attempt in 1826 to establish a federal regime in Chile, Jose Joaquín Mora, a Spanish liberal, wrote a new constitution in 1828. But by 1831, the conservatives and the *estanqueros* had seized power, and in the spring of that year, a "grand constituent convention" was summoned to subdue the populist, anti-aristocratic, anticlerical dialect of the 1828 constitution.

2.2 The Conservative 1833 Constitution

The new constitution that emerged in May 1833, written by a nonelected body, was oriented toward a strong presidency. The president of the country was allowed two consecutive five-year terms, and the office held extensive power over the cabinet, judiciary, public administration, and armed forces. The 1833 constitution was markedly centralist, with political hegemony residing in the capital city of Santiago, a feature that still defines Chile's highly centralized administrative and political system today.

According to official history, Chile emerged as one of South America's most stable, politically advanced, and educated (by the standards of that time) nations, one in which democratic government was largely the rule. Nonetheless, this is largely a myth as less than 5 percent of the total population voted in elections during most of the nineteenth century. In order to vote, people had to be literate and own property. In addition, representatives (*diputados*) and senators had to have incomes at a certain level above the national average.

It is important to note that the Chilean military actively influenced the critical foundational moments of the modern Chilean state – the approval of new constitutions in 1833, 1925, and 1980. In fact, these constitutions that lay the basis for the subsequent social contracts prevailing in the country, rather than stemming from orderly democratic and popular deliberation, emerged from authoritarian rule or followed military insurrections and were surrounded by different degrees of latent or open violence. No constitution of the Republic of Chile has been written by elected bodies. In the only case in which the constitution was drafted by an elected convention, in September 2022, the electorate ultimately rejected it.[6]

---

[6] See Salazar (2009) and Rosas and Benítez (2009).

2.3 Bimetallism, Inconvertibility Crises, and Fiscal Money

In the second half of the nineteenth century, Chile had a bimetallic monetary system based on full convertibility between the local currency and gold or silver. In addition to copper, vellon (a metal alloy of copper, nickel, and zinc) was used for minting coins of low denomination.

The monetary laws of 1851 and 1860 enabled a handful of commercial banks – the so-called *bancos de emisión* – to print paper money. The 1860 financial law in particular comprised very light bank regulation and required banks to hold modest capital-to-lending ratios.

A key variable of the monetary regime was the parity between gold and silver, the "mint ratio" set by the Casa de Moneda (a government-run coinage house). Misalignments between the official mint ratio and the market ratio could result either in the scarcity of lower-denomination coins based chiefly on silver (and copper and vellon) or in the scarcity of higher-denomination gold coins. The scarcity of low-denomination coins was predominant at the time.[7]

During wars such as the conflicts with Bolivia and Peru, the Chilean government borrowed from commercial banks to cover the increased fiscal deficits associated with higher military spending. The bimetallic monetary regime lasted until 1878 and was followed by a period of currency inconvertibility until 1895, when Chile entered a short-lived gold standard regime that lasted until 1898. A long-standing controversy on which monetary regime was better for Chile in the nineteenth and early twentieth centuries was between the *oreros*, those favoring the gold standard (*oro* means gold in Spanish) and the *papeleros*, those favoring inconvertible paper money (*papel* means paper).[8]

In 1898, "fiscal (paper) money," bills issued by a government agency (no central bank yet existed), became the only authorized currency sanctioned as legal tender. Fiscal money displaced commercial bank currency as commercial banks were forbidden to issue liabilities in the form of currency.

On the political front, 1891 was a crisis year that challenged the authority of President José Manuel Balmaceda, a progressive leader who promoted the building of railways, roads, and schools and wanted the Chilean state to have more control over nitrate production and revenues. The administration started to face opposition from conservative groups in alliance with British investors in mining and finance.[9] Balmaceda's opposition accused him of overstepping legal boundaries by issuing an official budget that the congress deemed was beyond the mandate of his office, and most congressional members signed an act of deposition against the president.

---

[7] A full monetary history of Chile until the early twentieth century is Subercaseaux (1922).
[8] See Fetter (1931) and Subercaseaux (1922).   [9] Ramírez Necochea (1958).

The two sides (those loyal to Balmaceda and the opposition) eventually squared off when congressional leaders formed an organized resistance with the support of the navy. With the army remaining faithful to the executive, the two sides (the president versus the parliament, and the army versus the navy) engaged in a bloody seven-month civil war in which, after the death of some 10,000 combatants, the conservatives emerged as victors over President Balmaceda, who committed suicide rather than submit to trial.

Although the 1833 constitution remained in place, congressional leaders established a stylized parliamentary system in which the national parliament indirectly controlled the reins of government by enacting periodical laws (*leyes periódicas*) that took power away from the executive branch by controlling presidential nominations, the appointment of cabinet members, and, perhaps most importantly, the budget. The president remained the head of state, but with largely weakened powers. The parliamentarian period coincided also with a period of increasing social demands by labor unions and organized social movements, following internal migration from the decaying nitrate fields in the north to urban centers in the rest of the country. This period entertained social demands for better housing, less burdensome labor conditions, children and women's rights, and more progressive social legislation.[10]

The parliamentary system remained in place until 1924, when the populist liberal president, Arturo Alessandri Palma, who had been elected in 1920, was ousted in a military coup by the September junta.[11] However, just four months later, the September junta was ousted in another military coup by the January junta, an effort by the supporters of the January junta to forestall what they believed was a massive conservative power shift in the country. After the coup d'état, Alessandri was returned to power, promising the masses that he would implement social reform and enable the new constitution of 1925, which ceded greater powers back to the president's office.

2.4 The More Progressive Constitution of 1925

In 1924, social discontent with the elitist politics of the conservative populist Alessandri government and the continued negation of broad social rights for almost 100 years prompted young officers from the army to demand political change in a movement called *ruido de sables* (that is, they rattled their sabers in protest). Their demands for political reform led to the writing of a new constitution, but not directly by a constitutional assembly as was envisaged at the start.

---

[10] See Solimano (2021, chapter 4).
[11] Arturo Alessandri was the father of Jorge Alessandri Rodríguez, who was president between 1958 and 1964.

In fact, a constitutional assembly of workers and intellectuals (*la constituyente chica*) with 1,250 delegates from different provinces, social organizations, and political parties representing working- and middle-class people gathered and opened discussions for shaping a new constitution to be followed by a broader constitutional assembly. After hesitation and doubts, President Alessandri, under pressure from the military, refrained from calling a constitutional assembly and appointed, in a rather Chilean political tradition, a small commission to draft the new constitution and called a plebiscite to ratify it.[12]

The 1925 constitution stated the official separation of church and state, which was the culmination of the gradually eroding political and economic power of the Roman Catholic Church and also provided legal recognition of workers' right to organize themselves into labor unions, promoted the social welfare of all citizens, and enabled the state to restrict private property for the public good. In addition, it established a balance between the executive, parliament, and judiciary, increasing the powers of the president in relation to the bicameral parliament in place after the defeat of the liberal administration of President Balmaceda in the Chilean Civil War of 1891. It created the basis for more modern social legislation and broadening of social rights.

The new constitution extended presidential terms from five to six years but did not allow consecutive terms. It established a system of proportional representation for parties with slates of candidates up for the parliament. The government was divided into four branches in descending order of power: the president, the legislature, the judiciary, and the comptroller general, the latter authorized to judge the constitutionality of all public-sector actions, the correct use of public property, and transparency in management of the fiscal budget. With some amendments the constitution of 1925 survived until the military coup of September 1973.

In 1925, as part of structural monetary and fiscal reforms, the Banco Central de Chile was established along with the superintendency of banks, the office of the general comptroller, a modernization of the fiscal budget, and a return to the gold standard. American professor Edward W. Kemmerer advised the Chilean government on these matters.

2.5 The Great Depression, Import Substitution Development, and Chronic Inflation

The Great Depression of the 1930s hit Chile very hard, with GDP contracting by 46 percent between 1929 and 1932.[13] In 1931, the gold standard introduced at the time of the Kemmerer reforms was abandoned and an array of foreign exchange controls and multiple exchange rates was

---

[12] See Grez Toso (2009).   [13] Solimano (2020).

put in place to save international reserves that were declining due to deterioration in terms of trade, fall in export volumes, and cuts in foreign lending. A severe external balance of payments deficit developed that called for a cut in imports induced by recession. At political level, the disarray the Great Depression brought about in Chile was reflected in the fall of the authoritarian government of Carlos Ibañez del Campo followed by a short succession of different presidents.

The situation stabilized with the reelection of Alessandri, who headed the government from 1932 until 1938. Unlike its populist stance of the early to mid-1920s, the second Alessandri government was rather conservative politically in the period 1932–8 and gave strong emphasis to fiscal consolidation in the economy.

After recovering from the Great Depression and restoring a degree of political and social stability, Chile, like other Latin American countries, embarked on an ISI strategy to reduce external dependence on imports and foreign investment and promote domestic industrialization. The ISI strategy Chile followed from the early 1940s to the early 1970s created productive activities that enjoyed import protection from tariffs and other devices (quotas and preferential import arrangements for intermediate parts and capital equipment). The ISI strategy also came with expanded labor union membership in the public and industrial sectors. Labor unions were particularly active in the 1950s and 1960s as inflation eroded the purchasing power of wages.

The agrarian elite of landholders benefited from the ownership of large areas of land, which started to change with the launch of agrarian reform from the mid-1960s until 1973. The agrarian reform (1962–1973) permitted the redistribution of land ownership in favour of peasants and allowed peasant unionization. In the social arena, public policies were advancing toward increasing degrees of universality in the provision of social services within a general trend of rising inclusion of the middle and working classes through access to public education, public healthcare, housing, and social security schemes. Social rights were promoted through progressive legislation and labor codes improving universality but faced difficulties in reaching the very poor in rural areas and the marginalized in urban centers.

From 1938 to 1952, the Radical Party (a centrist, nonreligious, political party) held power through three presidents. The "radical party cycle" embarked on an ISI policy that created a sector of state-owned enterprises in copper, steel, energy, and other activities and established a mass-education program, a national healthcare system, and a pay-as-you-go social security system. A sort of renewed social contract developed that reached out to the middle and working classes. Chile maintained a relatively participatory and stable democracy during the period that could accommodate social movements and working-class organizations, chiefly the Central Unica de Trabajadores, a nationwide union operating in the industrial and service sectors, public enterprises, and other government agencies.

In 1952, Ibañez (a former general who had ruled as an autocrat between 1927 and 1931) won the presidential election. His presidency was marked by high inflation, labor unrest, and unstable politics. To solve Chile's economic difficulties, a group of US-based external consultants – the Klein–Saks Mission – recommended fiscal austerity, monetary restraint, wage repression, and opening trade.

The results of the Ibañez stabilization policy were not encouraging and the new conservative government of Jorge Alessandri elected in 1958 departed from orthodox demand-based stabilization and launched an anti-inflationary program centered on a fixed exchange rate parity between the Chilean peso and the US dollar. The program also included cuts in import tariffs (to cheapen import goods) and financial deregulation (private dollar-denominated accounts could be opened in domestic banks). Inflation declined but at the cost of creating, after a certain period, a large balance of payments deficit and financial vulnerability following the dollarization of liabilities in the banking system. The program was abandoned in 1962 and Jorge Alessandri finished his presidential term in 1964.

A "new" political party emerged that was electorally important during the period – the Christian Democrats, a group of largely disaffected conservatives and social Christians who wished to move Chile toward more centrist policies and promote social reforms. The party candidate, Eduardo Frei Montalva, was elected president in 1964 with the votes of the right to stop the left's candidate, Allende, who was running for his third time. Frei was elected by a broad majority but governed with the official support of the Christian Democratic Party only. It deepened agrarian reform, undertook the "Chileanization" of US-owned copper interests (agreed semi-nationalization), and pursued more inclusive credit policies. Along with these reforms came a progressive social agenda that included the emergence of a loose social alliance of urban dwellers (*pobladores*), peasants (*campesinos*), students, and labor union members, as well as clear policies to expand educational opportunities to the poor. The political economy of the 1960s was characterized by higher demands for democratization, reflected in the growing participation of various groups in national decisions and the acceleration of agrarian reform. In short, Frei's administration was responsible for initiating many progressive reforms in Chilean society (several of them reversed after the military coup of September 1973), including *promoción popular* (social promotion), *reforma agraria* (agrarian reform), *reforma educacional* (education reform), and *juntas de vecinos* (neighborhood associations) among the main projects.

The Frei government's economic stabilization policy departed from the exchange rate–based stabilization of the first period of the Alessandri Rodriguez government and implemented a multifront strategy composed of incomes policy based on wage guidelines, a managed (*programada*) exchange rate policy (following a path of preannounced decreasing peso devaluations), and the setting of monetary targets by the central bank, all consistent with a target inflation rate.

Although economic growth in 1960–9 averaged a respectable 4.9 percent annually (with average per capita GDP growth at 2.5 percent), inflation remained stubborn at around 25 percent annually, and the country experienced chronic balance of payments deficits and fiscal imbalances.[14] Moreover, as the second half of the 1960s began to unfold, the impetus of social movements seen early in the Frei government, augmented by the winds of social unrest blowing across Latin America (the Cuban revolution was influential at that time) and in other parts of the world, was giving vent to growing calls for greater democratization and popular participation in government policy. In Chile, it was the start of more significant labor activism, fueled by the current capitalist mode of economic organization – the unwanted presence of foreign-owned enterprises in the country, a fatigued ISI policy that discouraged exports and was thus inimical to growth, chronic inflation, and persistent income and wealth inequality. All of these began to drive Chile toward the left-leaning (pro-working-class) elements of presidential politics. At the same time, the accelerated pace of democratization, popular participation, and economic redistribution was being resisted by the upper-income groups within Chilean society, creating social tension.

2.6 The Chilean Way to Socialism: The Allende Government of 1970–1973

In 1970, Salvador Allende, a candidate of the Unidad Popular (UP) (an alliance of socialists, communists, and small parties such as the Movimiento de Acción Popular Unitaria [MAPU] and Izquierda Cristiana [Christian Left]) rode a left-wing surge to win the election, but with only 36.3 percent of the popular vote (the congress then ratified the election). President Allende quickly began implementing policies around a program called the "Chilean way to socialism," in which a transition to Chilean-style socialism – different from the socialism of the Soviet Union and Cuba – would be accomplished through legal and constitutional means. To break up the concentration of economic power in the

---

[14] Ffrench-Davis (1973) provides a detailed reference of economic policies adopted in 1950–70. Meller, (1996) contains a long-term overview of the Chilean economy from the nineteenth century. Bitar (1979), Larraín and Meller (1990), and Vuskovic (1993) provide analyses from different perspectives of the Allende experience.

capitalist class, large industrial holdings and banks were brought in the hands of the state in the so-called *area social* that, according to Allende's electoral platform, would be composed by no more than ninety large enterprises that were wielding monopolistic power in industry and that provided the material base of the dominant economic elites. The foreign-owned copper mines were nationalized by law with unanimous vote in the parliament, and agrarian reform was accelerated.

Politically, President Allende himself (a former minister in previous Popular Front governments, a senator for many years, and a president of the Senate in the 1960s) sought a "neo-socialist" agenda in which economic reform in support of the working class would coexist with policies that would seek to transform and deepen the political system of representative democracy that was considered elitist and devoid of popular participation but still respected. Despite intense disagreement between the moderate (the communists) and more radical elements (the socialists) of the UP coalition over political strategy and elements of the economic program, the UP's official platform did not call for central planning or the dictatorship of the proletariat.

The Allende government had active support from intellectuals as well as from labor unions, peasant organizations, left-wing political parties, and progressive middle-class organizations. Although inflation accelerated sharply in 1972–3, the labor union movement, in general, supported the Allende government (1970–3) and the head of the Nationwide Labor Confederation became the minister of labor and social security in the UP government. Nonetheless, the economic crisis that erupted in 1972, resulting in high inflation, food shortages, strikes, and the stalling of growth, turned upper-middle-income groups and well-to-do households against the government, and even mobilized some labor unions in the copper sector. This climate of internal division eventually also reached the armed forces, traditionally respectful of civilian democratic rule, and led them, with support from the US government, to stage a ruthless military coup in September 1973.

The Allende period of transition to democratic socialism became more polarized. Economic elites opposed nationalization policies and agrarian reform. They resented the attempt to change Chile's economic and political structure away from the traditional power elites and toward the working classes.

A weak point of President Allende's strategy – besides underestimating the US reaction, under the Republican administration of Richard Nixon, to a socialist government in the Southern Cone – was the undertaking of over-expansionary macroeconomic policies based on a strong fiscal impulse, a simultaneous large increase in wages to stimulate aggregate demand, and a price freeze that created macro imbalances that were hard to finance given shortages of foreign exchange. As mentioned before, the UP government went on to nationalize the country's US-owned copper mines (as well as coal and steel), most private banks, and, beyond the original plan, almost 500 private firms and companies (including most of the country's textile firms, as well as US-owned International Telephone and Telegraph Company [IT&T]) were either formally nationalized or occupied by their workers. After a rapid increase in growth and employment in 1971, the result of the first set of policies was a fiscal deficit (financed by money creation), a zooming inflation rate (since 1972), product hoarding, a burgeoning black market, and instability both in the countryside (as peasants began seizing land held by wealthy landowners) and in urban areas (as workers tried seizing small and medium-size firms that were not included in the official nationalization program).

On the foreign front, US copper corporations, dissatisfied with nationalization terms, managed to mobilize the US government to cut multilateral funding to Chile from the International Monetary Fund (IMF) and the World Bank. The Church Report of the US Congress later confirmed that the Nixon administration through the Central Intelligence Agency (CIA) also engaged in political and economic destabilization of the Allende government and favored the military coup of September 1973.[15]

The result was the flight of foreign capital, a cut in foreign aid, withdrawals of money from banks, financially stressed industries, hyperinflation, the exhaustion of international reserves, and a fiscal deficit of nearly 25 percent of GDP in late 1973; in effect, the economy was sabotaged and the nation was increasingly divided, with strikes by labor, a disaffected middle class that was taking the brunt of the economic hardships, and a capitalist class that was afraid that Allende was laying the groundwork for a socialist country that would expropriate the capitalist class of its economic and political power.

In fact, evidence suggests that Allende tried placating those who were being alienated from the center of politics – including the wealthy capitalists and the military. One of his appointments was Pinochet, whom Allende named commander in chief of the Chilean armed forces in August 1973 because Pinochet, a disciplined soldier, conscientiously followed the president's orders – including helping to curb a failed military uprising on July 29, 1973 (the *Tanquetazo*) – when other military personnel, most of whom were middle class, were expressing their dissatisfaction with the left-wing government. However, both the Supreme Court and the parliament had denounced what they believed was Allende's usurpation of government power, and Pinochet adroitly surmised where true power resided. Although Allende still believed in

---

[15] Solimano (2012a, 2012b).

Pinochet's loyalty when first learning of the rebellion by the armed forces, Pinochet saw that he was just one step away from controlling Chile.

2.7 Neoliberal Economics under Pinochet's Repressive Military Regime

On September 11, 1973, Pinochet led a four-man junta that seized control of the government, ousting Allende, who died in the assault, which included bombing by the Chilean air force on the presidential palace, La Moneda.[16] Pinochet's brutal repression of Allende supporters, workers, students, and progressive intellectuals in the weeks immediately following the coup – a practice maintained for years during his regime – is well documented. By most accounts, the number of citizens that his secret police, the National Intelligence Directorate (DINA), created in 1974, detained, imprisoned, tortured, or executed (including those who "disappeared") almost certainly extends beyond the figures cited by the Rettig Commission.[17]

The military regime, after an initial flirtation with nationalistic economic policies that reflected the historical leanings of the army in economic matters, started to experiment with neoliberal, free market economics. To help the Pinochet regime implement these policies, the military junta recruited into important decision-making positions a team of around twenty-five economics experts who were Chilean-born but trained at the University of Chicago School of Economics in the United States. Their agenda called for abolishing price controls, privatizing state enterprises, deregulating markets, reducing import tariffs to boost exports and cheapen imports, reducing the inflation rate by establishing macroeconomic discipline (through a drastic fiscal adjustment program in 1975 in which nearly 100,000 public employees were separated from the state sector in one year), restituting property to its former owners, and securing external credits.[18]

The free market economic agenda of the military regime affected traditional industrialists who had flourished in the ISI period. Neoliberal policies had the

---

[16] Parts of this and subsequent sections are based on Solimano (2012a).

[17] The Rettig Commission was a nontrial "truth" tribunal established by the first democratically elected president after Pinochet's reign, Patricio Aylwin, to investigate human rights violations under the regime, and specifically "disappearances after arrest, executions, and torture leading to death committed by government agents or people in their service, as well as kidnappings and attempts on the life of persons carried out by private citizens for political reasons" (cited in Hayner, 2001).

[18] Ironically, however, despite movement away from state intervention – one of the main pillars of the neoliberal economic growth paradigm – Pinochet did not return the copper industry and other important mineral resources to foreign ownership and, in fact, put them under state control with a special clause that directed part of the profits of the copper industry to the Chilean armed forces. The state company, Codelco, was founded in 1976.

support of a class of new owners who acquired public enterprises at low cost, and of financial intermediaries who reaped big benefits from banking deregulation. Workers could not effectively oppose privatization policies and massive layoffs occurred in the public sector as unions were severely restricted in their activities. A new dynamic sector was the agroindustry for export, which created additional support groups for opening trade. This sector benefited from more competitive real exchange rates and lower tariffs, and from policies adopted in the 1960s to promote forestry, fishing, and fruit planting.

The Chilean experiment with neoliberal economics drew support from two champions of free market economics: Milton Friedman and Friedrich Von Hayek. Friedman backed these reforms by lecturing himself in Chile in 1975 and prepared a full policy report that he personally delivered to General Pinochet, advocating that a free market would bring a free society and recommending "shock treatment" (the story goes that Friedman could have risked losing the Nobel Prize in economics in 1976 due to his close association with the despised General Pinochet).[19] Later on, in 1981, Hayek – famous for writing *The Road to Serfdom* in the 1940s – also visited Chile and supported the ongoing free market revolution carried out by a repressive military regime. Hayek had previously courted authoritarian leader Oliveira-Salazar of Portugal on constitutional issues.[20] Hayek's closeness with right-wing authoritarian leaders undermines his allegiance to "free societies."

Chile indeed soon became the fastest-growing economy in South America, although the economy was also plagued by high unemployment and growing inequality. After successive stabilization plans combining shock treatment (entailing sharp cuts in aggregate demand and currency devaluation) and exchange rate–based stabilization by 1978, annual inflation had been cut to approximately 30 percent. Trade liberalization, privatization, fiscal adjustment, and market liberalization policies dominated the policy agenda of the second half of the 1970s. In the two years leading up to mid-1981, there was a real appreciation of the exchange rate against a fixed parity of 39 Chilean pesos per US dollar and ample inflows of foreign capital. Investment and consumption boomed, and banks were lending heavily both to other banks and to economic conglomerates still in fragile shape. In the late 1970s, the economy at last started to show some positive figures: GDP grew an average of 8.1 percent per year in 1977–81. Exports grew at 16 percent on average in that period, faster than ever before, and reached historical levels in 1980, a level matched only seven years later. Further, the fiscal budget ran consecutive surpluses in the period after at least fifteen years of deficits and the Central Bank built international reserves as

---

[19] Kornbluh (2013).   [20] Corey (2013).

well, peaking in 1980 at $4 billion (all dollars cited in this Element are US dollars). Inflation was cut from 340 percent in 1975 (174 percent in 1976, 63.5 percent in 1977) to 9.5 percent in 1981. Macroeconomic numbers had improved, but not on all relevant fronts.

However, although the exchange rate–based stabilization program between 1978 and 1982 reduced inflation, this effort was far from costless, showing the inherent difficulties of reducing chronically high inflation. In fact, other economic indicators such as employment and the solvency of the financial sector were hurt by accumulated overvaluation of the Chilean peso – a tool used to reduce the local price of imported goods and dampen internal inflation – as it led to a loss of competitiveness of the economy along with distorted patterns of credit allocation to risky customers.

As early as 1981, the economy was entering a severe economic and financial crisis.[21] The current account deficit had climbed to a record 14 percent of GDP, showing the existence of a very large external imbalance, and the risk profile of banks' loan portfolios increased in the face of insufficient banking regulation and monitoring by the authorities. The combined effect of a reduction of an unsustainable deficit in the current account of the balance of payments, adverse terms of trade and external interest rates shocks, along with the cutoff on domestic credit by a largely bankrupt banking system and the reduction of real wages following the depreciation of the peso, all led to a sharp decline in private demand for consumption and investment during 1982.

The cut in aggregate demand and plunging investment brought about a rapid decline in output and income, primarily in 1982, but bottoming out in late 1983. Between the peak level of the third quarter of 1981 and the bottom level of the same quarter of 1983, per capita income was at 75 percent of its level in the late 1960s, and the cumulative decline in GDP in the two years was 16 percent. Inflation had itself almost more than doubled from its low level of 9.5 percent in the twelve months prior to December 1981. The promising economic outlook of the preceding years turned into an economic and financial crash.

A crisis in the banking sector quickly ensued, with recurrent currency devaluations and serious external debt-servicing problems. Many small and medium-scale firms drowned in debt or went bankrupt, with an ensuing destruction of organizational capital and jobs. With the decline in real wages and an escalation in the cost of living, the share of absolute poverty increased. In turn, the open unemployment rate skyrocketed to around 20 percent of the labor force by 1982. Moreover, free markets under Pinochet again came at a dear human

---

[21] References of that period are Corbo and Solimano (1991), Edwards and Edwards (1991), Ffrench-Davis (2002), Foxley (1983), Meller (1996), Solimano (1993, 1999), and Solimano and Pollack (2007).

price, and they made other countries in the area and those who governed them hesitant to adopt market reforms as they equated economic freedom with political authoritarianism and social inequality.

The economic crisis and depression triggered immediate pressures on the government to change its policies. Nonetheless, the government's initial reaction as early as 1981 was to reiterate its commitment to free market policies and thus to refrain from intervening, maintaining a policy known as "automatic adjustment" – resemblant of the early Great Depression policies in the United States in the 1930s when Herbert Hoover was president – which was basically depression-induced price deflation. That course had to be abandoned when the severity of the crisis soon became quite clear.

Besieged by events, in June 1982, the military government decided to abandon the fixed exchange rate policy of 39 pesos per US dollar that had been followed for three years and was the cornerstone of its stabilization program. This decision implied a devaluation of the Chilean peso; in the next three months, it depreciated from 39 to 63 Chilean pesos per US dollar. This policy was supposed to benefit exporters and import-competing sectors, but it also sharply increased the foreign debt-servicing burden in local currency and deteriorated the balance sheets of firms that had borrowed in dollars (but whose revenues were in pesos in commitment to the fixed exchange rate), probably believing that the fixed exchange rate system implemented by the government would last forever.

To control the unfolding financial crisis, the government instituted, first, a large debt relief program based on a preferential exchange rate for debtors in dollars, and, second, took over the management of several banks in distress with a large stock of nonperforming loans. These financial relief programs were financed with the issue of treasury and central bank bonds to be placed with domestic investors, particularly the new private pension funds emerging from the privatization of the social security system in 1981. These policies were supported with loans from the IMF, the World Bank, and the Inter-American Development Bank (IDB). The social consequences were dire.[22]

Despite the economic and social distress brought about by the Pinochet government's policies – and its tardy response to it – the government retained its repressive hold over Chile. Direct military rule starting in 1973 was extended by nondemocratic plebiscite in 1978; in 1980, another plebiscite (also with dubious transparency and competitiveness) approved a new constitution that gave Pinochet sweeping executive power until 1990. This constitution was not

---

[22] Solimano and colleagues (2000) discuss the array of social consequences ensuing from the policies to deal with the crisis of the early 1980s.

prepared by a constitutional assembly but by an ad hoc commission and the state council that in 1980 presented a constitutional text to the military junta. The junta, after some revisions, gave thirty days for calling a plebiscite for popular ratification of the new constitution.

2.8 Pinochet's Constitution of 1980 Tried to Undermine the Republic

The constitution of 1925 fell prey to the military coup that overthrew the Allende government on September 11, 1973. A new constitution was drafted by the Ortuzar Commission, appointed after the 1973 coup; it was then modified by the *junta de gobierno* (military junta) between 1978 and 1980. On the seventh anniversary of Pinochet's military takeover, the government issued a controlled plebiscite in which the new constitution was "approved" by Chilean voters in the absence of electoral registers, free press, and other constitutional guarantees. As of 2023, this constitution was still in place with several modifications.

The 1980 constitution legally sanctioned three major tenets of neoliberalism – placing supreme value on private ownership of the means of production; promoting the "minimal state," severely restricting the state in its economic role as producer (except for the copper industry, the main provider of funding for the military); and clamping down severely on labor rights. The constitution embedded the notion of a *protected democracy* by making the armed forces the "guarantors of the institutional order."

During an eight-year period (after 1980), the junta, via the National Security Council, would be allowed to enact "temporary provisos" to maintain an "orderly" transition, and it was immune from any standard democratic controls or social oversight, including a clause that prevented any civilian president from removing the commander in chief of the army, navy, and air force without the consent of the National Security Council (this proviso was nullified after the constitutional reforms of 2005, whereby a civilian president can effect removal only after congressional approval). In addition, the upper house of parliament, the Senate, was to include eleven nonelected members.

After years of acute domestic social protest entailing street demonstrations and pot-hitting at home in concerted days and other means – all severely repressed by the army and the secret police, particularly in 1983 and 1984 – and under international pressure, Pinochet opted for another plebiscite in 1988 to extend his rule even further for another eight years. But the emergence of a broad coalition of leftist and centrist parties compelled a record 92 percent of the population to register to vote and swept in a coalition that came to be known as the Concertación with a commanding "No" vote against Pinochet.

2.9 Chile's Post-Pinochet Democracy

After the plebiscite of October 1988 rejected General Pinochet's bid to remain in power for another eight years, on December 14, 1989, the first truly free and open election in nearly twenty years took place. Elected were most new members of a two-chamber parliament, as well as a new president, Christian Democrat Patricio Aylwin, the candidate of the center–left Concertación coalition, who received 55 percent of the vote.

The post-Pinochet political system in the 1990s and 2000s centered around two big coalitions, "center–left" and "center–right," that largely excluded social movements and the political parties that did not belong to these two coalitions. This brought political "stability" to the country but also restricted political representation of alternative positions and was ultimately functional to the continuity of the neoliberal economic model within a low-intensity democracy by narrowing the national debate and restricting the admissible alternatives to the status quo.

President Aylwin served from 1990 to 1994 in what would be considered a transitional phase. As part of the late 1980s talks between the Pinochet government and the political opposition about the transition from the military regime to a democratic government, the opposition to Pinochet was able to assume power by agreeing to support the fundamentals of the neoliberal economic model in place and refrain from actively pursuing judicial prosecution of those ultimately responsible for the massive violations of human rights that took place under the military regime (Pinochet remained commander in chief of the army until March 1998) following his arrest in London.

An unbalanced social partnership between (strong) capital and (weakened) labor was encouraged amidst a policy framework favorable to private investment along with a cooperative, deferential attitude from what remained as organized labor – which had survived the active repression and legal changes oriented to reduce the power of the labor union movement in the 1973–89 period (Pinochet regime). In the context of a fragile, recovering democracy, labor demands, including further unionization, higher wages, and more extensive labor rights, were *not* encouraged. Ensuring social control of labor and enabling high profits for the corporate sector were the policy priorities of the center–left government at the time, to support private investment.

At the same time, the Aylwin administration, more conscious that social conditions had to improve, did raise taxes at the outset to fund social programs and finance a boost in social spending to reverse the social deterioration inherited from the military period. The administration raised minimum wages, increased monetary subsidies to the poor, and provided more money to chronically underfunded public healthcare and educational systems. It also devoted fiscal resources to revamping public infrastructure – ports, roads, and highways – which had deteriorated after years of public investment neglect.

Macroeconomic policies in the 1990s were targeted at accommodating higher social spending while also reducing inflation, in addition to taxing short-term capital inflows and reducing public external debt. However, a structural rebalancing of the distribution of income between capital and labor was avoided, a move functional to the continuation of the neoliberal model brought by Pinochet and the Chicago Boys in the preceding decade.

In the next election in December 1993, Christian Democrat Eduardo Frei Ruiz-Tagle, the son of President Eduardo Frei Montalva, led the Concertación coalition to victory with a clear majority of votes, at 58 percent. During Pinochet's regime, Frei had been instrumental in establishing the Free Elections Committee, and he campaigned actively for the "No" vote to the 1988 plebiscite to return to democratically elected governments.

In his administration, President Frei Ruiz-Tagle, himself a former entrepreneur, leaned toward the neoliberal paradigm by privatizing the water sector, closing coal mines, and overseeing the integration of the Chilean economy by integrating it more fully into the international community. He signed free trade treaties with Canada, Mexico, and various Central American countries, and during his tenure, Chile became a member of MERCOSUR (Southern Common Market), the World Trade Organization, and the Asia-Pacific Economic Cooperation (APEC). Still, he kept an eye also on the social landscape. In running for presidential office, he pledged to alleviate poverty and to put more women into public office – indeed, he appointed three women to his cabinet. In addition, he was more generous in the minimum wage policy followed under his government and tried to undertake countercyclical fiscal policies to protect employment and cope with the aftermath of the Asian crisis in Chile in 1998–9.

In 2000, socialist candidate Ricardo Lagos was elected president. Perhaps to show that a post-Allende socialist could take power and avert hints (or ghosts) of returning socialism and eventual anti-neoliberalism to Chile, President Lagos actively courted representatives of big business and high finance, dampened the potential activism of organized labor, and postponed changes in labor legislation. He also moderated environmental demands from ecological groups, and although he presented legislation to remove several provisos of the constitution of 1980, he fell short of calling for a referendum to undertake comprehensive reform and rewrite the constitution approved under Pinochet.

Critical democratic reforms that President Frei Montalva had proposed already in 1980, before his death in 1981 – a death recently proved masterminded by the Pinochet regime and other leaders of the opposition to Pinochet in the

1980s – such as the election of a constitutional assembly to draft a new constitution for Chile were *not* in the cards for the Lagos administration. A constitutional assembly would have drafted a new constitution and after popular ratification would have replaced, with broader political legitimacy, the 1980 constitution approved under Pinochet. However, Lagos did not follow this course of action. The new constitution was postponed indefinitely.

Still Lagos did introduce some social reforms, including a reformed public healthcare bill to extend coverage for several chronic illnesses to working- and middle-class people. In turn, he devoted important efforts to upgrade and modernize physical infrastructure with strong private-sector participation through user fee schemes. Tilting to economic orthodoxy, Lagos furthered conservative fiscal policies by adopting an explicit rule to run a structural fiscal surplus and achieved a further reduction in inflation. Furthermore, the Lagos administration suspended the tax on short-term capital inflows and supported a floating exchange rate regime with minimal Central Bank intervention.

In 2005, more than fifty constitutional reforms were approved by the parliament – but were not ratified by popular referendum – to eliminate some of the remaining, more undemocratic areas of the constitution such as ending the positions of nonelected senators and senators for life, phasing out the prohibition of the president from removing the commander in chief of the armed forces, reducing the president's term of office from six to four years, and diminishing the powers of the National Security Council. These reforms led President Lagos to state (controversially) that Chile's transition to democracy was completed. A true change would have been the drafting of a new constitution by a democratically elected constitutional assembly sanctioned, in turn, by popular vote.

In March 2006, the Socialist Party candidate, Michelle Bachelet, assumed the presidency as the fourth administration from the Concertación. Ms. Bachelet, who was put in jail in the 1970s and then exiled for resistance to the Pinochet regime, was the first – and only – woman president in the history of Chile. She initially tried to rule under the banner of a "citizen's government" and gender "parity government," meaning independence from the dictates of the ruling bodies of political parties that formed the coalition supporting her government and equal representation of men and women in cabinet appointments. These two purposes, independence from political parties and gender equality at the ministerial level, were relaxed later in her administration.

On the economic front, she appointed a neoliberal finance minister and strongly empowered him – regarding the rest of the cabinet and the political parties backing her government – with the double aim of keeping public finances in order (or in surplus) and to resist pressures to change the prevailing economic model coming from disaffected sectors of the Concertación, the labor movement, environmental groups, and pro-redistribution constituencies. In addition, this appeased potential challenges from big business organizations, which were very powerful in Chile. Her main (partial) social reform was of the social security system by creating a noncontributory "pension floor" that extended universal pensions payments and rights to all eligible citizens.

Nonetheless, reflecting the power of economic conglomerates in Chile, the Bachelet pension reforms of 2008–9 maintained virtually intact the controversial privatized pension system based on personal capitalization and run by for-profits pension management companies, the Administradoras de Fondos de Pensiones (AFP), that managed assets equivalent to around two-thirds of annual GDP. This privatized pension system is for the civilian population as members of the armed forces belong to a state-funded system that pays much higher pensions than the private system.[23]

In the first three years of Bachelet's tenure, Chile enjoyed a spectacular surge in copper prices, but economic growth remained relatively modest. The choice was to save the bonanza generating a current account surplus in the balance of payments and a large fiscal surplus on the order of 7–8 percent of GDP. Later, Chile was hit by the effects of the financial crash of 2008 in the United States and Europe, leading to a contraction in economic activity of 1.7 percent in 2009 and an increase in unemployment to nearly a million workers. Nevertheless, Chile avoided a banking crisis and the financial crash in the advanced economies worked their impact mainly through trade, capital inflows, and the real side of the economy. The savings made by the government and placed in assumedly safe financial assets in the United States during the bonanza years allowed the Bachelet government to implement countercyclical fiscal policies in 2008–9 without having to borrow abroad, dampening a perhaps more pronounced recession.

In retrospect, it is apparent that the first four center–left Concertación administrations (between March 1990 and March 2010) in some respects deepened the neoliberal model as they refrained from introducing progressive labor legislation and de-monopolizing sectors dominated by economic conglomerates. These governments were very aware of the need to maintain macroeconomic stability and adopted the fiscal and monetary orthodoxies of the time.

On the social front, the focus was primarily on poverty reduction and increased social protection for the most vulnerable groups initially (the extreme poor, the elderly, and women and children), but later, the "middle class" became

---

[23] See Solimano (2021).

a relative center of attention – for example, making available about $1 billion for home loans from the Stabilization Fund while at the same time putting in place an expensive (for the user of the loan) student loan system. In retrospect, it is apparent that Concertación policies never really tried to address the complex issue of the persistent, long-term inequality in income and wealth distribution; in turn, the center–left coalition allowed a big concentration of wealth in the hands of rich economic elites and horizontally integrated large economic conglomerates. These inequalities are among the highest, not only in Latin America, but also throughout the world.[24]

In 2010, a conservative government headed by businessman and Forbes list member billionaire Sebastian Piñera was elected president, marking the first post-Pinochet right-wing government (supposedly purged from the excesses of the General). Piñera managed to keep the economy growing at a respectable rate, maintained low inflation, and pushed an agenda of deepening the privatization of the economy regardless of social and environmental consequences. However, wealth inequality accentuated while the labor share in national income remained compressed and job vulnerability and labor's low influence in national politics accentuated.

In 2011, the Piñera government faced serious conflicts with the student movement demanding both the end of the system of paid education based on student debt and the launching of nonprofit educational reform that treated education as a social right rather than as a service delivered by markets. The government also contended with an active environmental movement opposing emblematic projects such as the building of a large water dam in the far south of the country (the Hydro-Aysen project).

In late 2013, former president Michelle Bachelet ran a second time for office and won. Her second government tried to strike a balance between maintaining a continuity in economic policies regarding the orientation of the prior two decades with needed reforms of the electoral system, women's participation, social equity, and other topics. An important piece of her economic agenda was tax reform oriented to collect more fiscal revenues to finance expanded social programs. Importantly, she promoted a process of constitutional public deliberations, the *cabildos*, that could have led to a new constitution replacing the one approved in 1980, which did not happen.

An important legacy of the Bachelet administration was bringing an end to the binominal system that had allowed, since the start of the transition to democracy in 1990, right-wing political parties to hold a sort of veto power in the congress but failed in her push for a new constitution. During the first

---

[24] See Fazio (2005) and Solimano (2007, 2012a, 2012b, 2021).

twenty-five years after the end of the military regime, legislation passed in the parliament had to be negotiated only with the center–right wing of the political spectrum as representatives from the left simply were not present in the parliament. As a result of this, political and economic legislation tilted toward more conservative positions. Despite Bachelet's accomplishments, the general feeling was that the modernizing and progressive reforming agenda of Bachelet II was not really completed during her term, chiefly due to political and ideological differences within her own coalition on the scope and breadth of those reforms.

The presidential election of 2017 brought again to government Sebastian Piñera. His second government was less guarded than his first administration regarding his neoliberal, pro-elite agenda and dismissed popular demands for more social equity, changes in labor laws, environmental protection, and a new constitution. However, contradictions within Chilean society mounted and eventually he faced an unprecedent social uprising – the *estallido social* – in October and November 2019, accompanied by massive protests, acute violence, and fire and destruction of property and public symbols. The trigger was a relatively modest rise in public transportation fares that sparked student protests, street fighting against police, and massive rallies across the country.

The Piñera government harshly repressed the social unrest. Police confrontations included tactics such as shooting rubber bullets into the eyes of protesters (many of them lost their eyes or were badly injured in their faces). This was a clear retreat from Piñera's previous stance of presenting himself as a new brand of conservative politician detached from Pinochet's tyrannical methods to contain social dissatisfaction.

Four international human rights organizations that sent mission teams to Chile – Amnesty International, the United Nations, the InterAmerican Human Rights Commission, and Human Rights Watch – all documented massive violations to human rights by the Piñera government during the October–November uprising. The protests came largely to an end when a broad agreement in mid-November 2019 comprising left-wing (excluding the Communist Party), centrist, and right-wing political parties agreed to electing a constitutional convention to draft a new constitution to be ratified by the population. The constitutional convention was to have gender parity and ensure representation of members of Indigenous population groups. However, it fell short from being a truly constitutional assembly in that rules of voting and other aspects were imposed by the existing parliament and the political agreement just mentioned rather than being defined by the members of the assembly.

After a year of deliberation between June 2021 and June 2022, the constitutional convention presented the draft of a new constitution whose main principles and provisos included the recognition of the Indigenous communities, egalitarian access to essential social services such as education, healthcare, housing, social security, care for the whole population including children and the elderly, and protection of the environment. These new principles represented a clear departure from the prevailing 1980 constitution that gave primacy to private property rights of productive wealth over labor and social rights and represented a clear retreat from the neoliberal model and the "minimal state" doctrine enshrined in the 1980 constitution.

Nonetheless, in the exit plebiscite, the proposed constitution was *rejected* by 62 percent of the electoral vote on September 4, 2022. The reasons for the majority are still matters of debate, but one of them can be highlighted: an ample and well-funded campaign by the right-wing press that controls the bulk of radio, TV, and newspapers in Chile. The mass media are largely owned by conservative economic conglomerates and generally hostile to progressive transformation of Chilean society. In addition, the preeminence of identity-based provisos in the proposed constitution regarding rights of the Indigenous population, gender parity, and decentralization apparently alienated important contingents of the population that could be more interested in material considerations and access to social services.

At the time of this writing, a process of formulating a new constitution has been defined by the congress and political parties. Three bodies will be involved during 2023 in writing a new constitution. These are the Expert Commission, responsible for creating an initial draft of the constitutional text selected by the national congress; the Constitutional Council, which will review and potentially modify the text chosen by citizens; and the Admissibility Technical Committee, which will act as an intermediary in cases where proposals for regulations may violate existing laws and will also be chosen by the congress.

2.10 Conclusion

Chilean economic development must be analyzed in terms of Chile's resources endowment. The nation is rich in natural resources, chiefly mining products, forestry and fishery. It also has a pattern of wide integration to the international economy, and its current social structure still reflects the legacies of colonial rule, and entrenched inequality with a powerful economic elite that manages to preserve its privileged socioeconomic role in society.

In the twentieth century, Chile suffered from chronic inflation, a high dependence on exports of nitrate and then copper, vulnerability to terms-of-trade shocks, and a cycle of a first rising and then falling share of the manufacturing industrial sector with deindustrialization prevailing in recent decades. In the nineteenth century, Chile tried the monetary system of bimetallism, free banking and commercial bank dominated money issuing, currency inconvertibility, the gold standard and fiscal money. In the 1920s, a central bank was created, accompanied by a return to the gold standard that was abandoned during the Great Depression of the 1930s. In the late twentieth and early twenty-first centuries, a new orthodoxy of independent central banking, inflation targeting, and fiscal rules replaced previous modalities of macroeconomic management.

The constitutional history of Chile is turbulent with several constitutions in the first two decades after independence, followed by a centralistic and authoritarian constitution approved in 1833, a more progressive constitution in 1925, and a constitution of 1980 printed to protect the neoliberal model and preserve the legacy of the Pinochet period. No constitution in republican Chile has been formulated by a fully elected constitutional assembly.

3 Patterns of Structural Transformation in Chile: Financialization and Deindustrialization

3.1 Introduction

Developed and developing countries have had different patterns of structural transformation (ST) in which the relative importance of different sectors varies over time and across nations. Historically during the nineteenth and twentieth centuries, while developed countries shifted away from primary/agricultural goods production toward manufacturing industries and then to services industries, some developing countries have shifted from agriculture to services (retail and trade) without developing a strong manufacturing sector – a process known as *premature deindustrialization* (Rodrik, 2016). The service sector is, in general, more productive than agriculture but is not, across the board, technology-intensive. On the contrary, a sizable manufacturing sector is strongly associated with a high degree of industrialization and therefore with more sustainable development.

The pattern of premature deindustrialization is not always the case. Korea, Taiwan, Singapore, and Finland created strong, technology-intensive sectors during their development processes. However, in the Latin American context, economies that have embraced trade liberalization, shrinking their industrial sector, cannot compete with low-cost goods coming from, say, China and other East Asian nations and have serious problems in developing a technologically advanced manufacturing sector. These countries were candidates for premature deindustrialization. Chile, which engaged in radical trade liberalization in the 1970s and 1980s, is an example of that tendency. The country had a respectable industrial base until the mid-1970s that included the manufacturing of car parts, electronics, and capital goods, but these activities have been sharply downsided with the arrival of the globalization process that Chile embraced in an uncritical way.

The process of ST often refers to the evolution of different productive sectors in the economy, measured by changes in sector shares of GDP, labor, and exports. Particularly, ST is often defined as the reallocation of economic activity between and within sectors toward higher-productivity activities (Herrendorf et al., 2014). The movement of labor to more productive activities is a driver of economic development as it increases overall productivity and efficiency in the economy. However, policy-induced labor reallocations can also reduce growth when labor is transferred from higher-productivity to lower-productivity sectors, as has been the case of Chile and Latin America (McMillan and Rodrik, 2011). Other concepts of structural change in society, more related to political economy configurations, can be used as well. They refer to changes in the relative power and influence of social actors such as entrepreneurs, financial oligarchies, foreign corporations, and labor that relate functionally to a determined economic structure and that are affected by ST. Chile experienced realignments in the influence of social actors when it switched from ISI to external opening and neoliberalism. In the latter regime, financial elites and exporters related to natural resources gained more importance displacing former entrepreneurial groups related to manufacturing products for the internal market. In turn, labor unions weakened and the bargaining power of labor diminished in significant ways.

The ST undertaken in Chile since the mid-to-late 1970s has been related to rapid trade liberalization and an *absence* of industrial policies, along with privatization and deregulation extended to both the productive and social sectors (education, healthcare, pensions, social housing). Chilean economic growth relies on the demand side, on the dynamism of exports, private investment, and private consumption; on the supply side, it relies mainly on the mining and services sectors. Despite a rising GDP trajectory with gains in GDP per capita over the past three to four decades, the country has undergone a steady process of *deindustrialization*, with the share of manufacturing in GDP reaching a historic low of 10 percent in 2018, a level resembling that of the early 1930s at the outset of the Great Depression. In contrast, in 1972, manufacturing was 25 percent of GDP (Lüders et al., 2016).

The neoliberal model promoted both trade liberalization and a government hands-off policy toward promotion of the industrial sector. Chile embraced that approach particularly in the "authoritarian neoliberal phase" of the Pinochet era (1973–89), although the absence of industrial policy and trade liberalization has continued in the "neoliberalism in democracy" phase since the early 1990s. Nonetheless, "pragmatic" neoliberalism during the first three decades of democratic restoration was not able to stop deindustrialization. Tellingly, industrial policy was never seriously adopted.

Chilean development patterns of the past few decades contain several features in need of substantive redirection to be suitable with the UNSDGs. From the mid-1970s up to now, the Chilean growth pattern has been based on the exploitation of natural resources (this trend comes from at least the nineteenth century), some of them exhaustible, in mining, with fishing and agroindustry that have been the leading sectors driving economic growth.

The more pragmatic (neoliberal) economic model since the 1990s has been accompanied by more public investment in the social sectors, infrastructure, and regional development, although its feature of persistent inequality of income and wealth and employment precarity has at times provoked serious social resistance. The episodes of social unrest of 2006, 2011, and 2019 are related to several factors, but employment vulnerability, expensive social services, and overall inequality ignite citizens' unsatisfaction. These problems have not been corrected in democracy and bouts of active social discontent have appeared.

On the supply side, growth has been mainly led by the strengthening of the services sector at the expense of the manufacturing sector. Services are labor-intensive but tend to have low productivity since they do not require significant investments in physical and human capital (some activities such as information technology may be the exception). On the contrary, the development of the manufacturing sector is linked to a more sustainable type of growth, high productivity, and job creation. In the early 1960s, the manufacturing sector contributed more than 30 percent of economic growth, much like the contribution of nonfinancial services.

What followed was a very rapid decline in the role of the industrial, manufacturing, and nonmanufacturing sectors, together with the scaling up of the impact of financial and nonfinancial services and mining. By the mid-1970s, the contribution of manufacturing to value-added growth was negative, while financial, nonfinancial, and mining services accounted for 90 percent of growth. After a gradual upturn of the contribution of the manufacturing sector to economic growth, it turned to a downward trend, reaching 15 percent in 2011 (see Figure 1).

3.2 Trends in Structural Transformation

The types of STs that allowed differentiating between developed and developing countries were, according to Solow (1956) and a vast literature on development patterns, related to sectoral development, factors of production, characteristics of

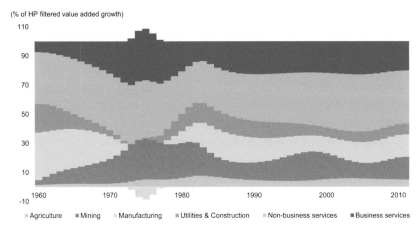

(% of HP filtered value added growth)

■ Agriculture   ■ Mining   ■ Manufacturing   ■ Utilities & Construction   ■ Non-business services   ■ Business services

Figure 1 Growth decomposition by sector, Chile, 1960–2011
(% of HP filtered value-added growth)

Note: business services: financial intermediation, renting, business activities; nonbusiness services: (a) wholesale and retail trade, repair of motor vehicles, motorcycles, and personal and household goods, hotels, and restaurants; (b) transport, storage, communications; (c) public administration, defense, education, healthcare, social work; and (d) other community, social, and personal service activities, and activities of private households

Source: Solimano and Zapata-Román (2022)

the financial system, and healthy dynamic influences – for example, a large proportion of workers who are highly qualified and employed in the formal sector and a diversified manufacturing industry that is larger than other sectors, such as agriculture or mining; also, strong public finances with low debt dependency that rely on direct taxes and provide social security, as well as diversified foreign trade in terms of products and recipient countries.[25] Finally, low poverty and posttax inequality, plus a well-developed financial system, high investment, and savings, are usually accompanied by slow population growth and high urbanization.

Sumner (2017), in a more contemporary understanding of STs, grouped these characteristics into three main areas. The first refers to sector aspects, or changes in the relative weight of the different productive sectors and their employment shares, toward higher productivity. Second, the factor aspects of ST are about the composition of the productive structure and productivity levels – drivers of economic growth. The third aspect relates to the characteristics of global integration in terms of trade and investment patterns. In the rest of this section, we will discuss the transitions Chile has experienced in relation to these three aspects.

---

[25] See Alisjahbana and colleagues (2022).

(% of HP filtered value added growth)

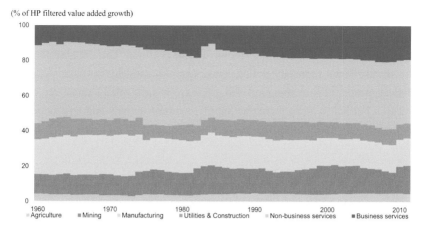

Figure 2 Value-added composition for Chile, 1960–2011
(% of value added)

Source: Solimano and Zapata-Román (2022)

3.2.1 Changes in the Chilean Economic Structure

Structural transformations are often described as the movement from agriculture to industry and services that are deemed more productive. In Chile, this trend has been seen in the displacement of employment away from agriculture but not in high value-added activities. Agriculture represented about 4 percent of value added from 1960 to 2000 and has been closer to 5 percent of the country's value added since (see Figure 2).

The size of the manufacturing sector is strongly associated with the degree of industrialization and therefore with more sustainable development. The economic policies of the military dictatorship that took power in September 1973 affected the trajectory of ST. These policies included privatization of public enterprises, rapid opening to international trade, devaluation of the local currency (peso chileno) and the curtailment of labor unions. Of these neoliberal reforms, trade liberalization was perhaps the one that most dramatically affected the country's productive structure.

Prior to 1974, the manufacturing industry enjoyed high tariff protection, which was gradually phased out, along with all import quotas, leaving flat import tariffs of 10 percent in 1979. Trade liberalization induced a significant change in relative prices in favor of agriculture, mining, and untradable goods, affecting the allocation of resources within the economy.[26] In the sharp recession

---

[26] Alvarez and Fuentes (2006); Contreras and Ffrench-Davis (2012).

of 1975, Chile's GDP dropped nearly 12 percent, with annual inflation exceeding 300 percent. The military government adopted that year a shock-treatment strategy to curb inflation, and the terms of trade declined. This entailed contractionary fiscal and monetary policy, along with a significant devaluation of the Chilean peso.[27] These measures did not have a substantial impact on sticky inflation but led to a sharp contraction of economic activity and a reduction of real wages. By 1975, industrial production had fallen by 28 percent.[28]

With the opening to international trade and the Latin American debt crises at the beginning of the 1980s, the manufacturing sector reached the lowest point of the decade in 1982 at 15.7 percent of total GDP. Manufacturing started to recover by the second half of the 1980s until 1994, but within a declining trend in the manufacturing sector's share of GDP in the beginning of the twenty-first century. The latest figures from the Chilean Central Bank show an even more pessimistic scenario, with the manufacturing sector falling to 8.6 percent of GDP in 2021.

Mining is a key productive sector for the country. Chile is the world's largest copper producer and owns one-third of the world's copper reserves, which are mainly used for electrical conduction. The share of the mining sector has represented, on average, 15 percent of the total economy since the mid-1970s. Fluctuations in the international price of copper have defined the trajectory of the sector, as this metal represents more than one-half of the country's total exports,[29] and the fall of the sector during the first half of the 1990s parallels the sharp drop in the international price of copper.[30] The boom in copper prices during the 2000s increased the profitability of the industry, attracting foreign investment, which helped grow the sector.[31]

The largest sector of the Chilean economy is services. To visualize the trends in this sector, we split it into two parts; the first comprises finance, insurance, real estate, and business services, and the second comprises nonbusiness services. The latter includes trade, restaurants, and hotels; transport, storage, and communication; and community, social, and personal services. The services sector has had rather stable participation in the total economy at 52–56 percent of the total value added from 1960 onward. However, its composition has changed over time: nonbusiness services have reduced its share in total output, while the financial services sector has steadily increased its relevance, reaching 20 percent of GDP by 2010. In other words, we observe a trend toward *financialization* of the Chilean economy that coincides also with *deindustrialization*.

---

[27] Ffrench-Davis (2018); Solimano (2012b).   [28] Jadresic (1986).

[29] During the period 1960–74, copper accounted, on average, for 80 percent of total exports. That figure dropped to about 60 percent in the period 1975–89 and fell to about 50 percent from the 1990s, on average.

[30] SONAMI (2019).   [31] OECD/UN (2018).

To summarize, the productive structure in Chile has experienced significant changes over the past fifty years. We can identify some trends in structural changes in sector shares. The first is the growth of the services and financial sector, as well as the mining sector. Services tend to be labor-intensive but not technology-intensive, and mining is technology-intensive but requires few workers, most of whom are highly qualified. The second trend is deindustrialization, shown by the shrinkage of the relative position of the manufacturing sector in aggregate output.

Industries such as textile, metal-mechanic, and shoe production declined sharply with trade liberalization in the mid-1970s and, later, with enhanced price competition from China and other East Asian markets. The ownership structure of productive assets strongly tilted toward the private sector due to the wave of privatization following the free market revolution of the mid-1970s. This trend of deindustrialization is worrisome and could negatively affect Chile's ability to achieve STs toward higher and more sophisticated levels of productive development and technological advance.

As Palma (2022) argues, Chile has the features of a "rentier economy" (based on natural resources, finance, and services) in which both the private sector and the state sector enjoy Ricardian rents by exploiting natural resources rather than being a "Schumpeterian economy" that relies on innovation and technological improvements concentrated in industry. Part of the concentration of income distribution at the top reflects the income-generating features of a rentier economy.

3.2.2 Changes in Employment Structure

Chile's employment structure has undergone drastic changes since 1960 following changes in its productive structure. In most sectors, we can distinguish inflexion points in the employment trajectories that coincide with both political and economic crises.

In 1960, three sectors represented 87 percent of total employment: nonbusiness services, agriculture, and manufacturing. Between 1960 and the mid-1970s, the employment share in agriculture fell steadily and was absorbed mainly by the manufacturing and nonbusiness services sectors. The period after the military coup (1973–5) marks a turning point for the manufacturing sector, which fell from 22 percent to 14 percent of total employment between 1973 and 1982. The declining trend in agriculture remained, and the nonbusiness services sector offset both shrinkages. With the economic crisis of 1981–2, GDP per capita fell by 17 percent and the unemployment rate doubled, reaching 20 percent in 1982.[32]

---

[32] Cowan and colleagues (2004).

After the debt crises of 1982–83, the economy recovered until the end of the military government in 1989. The financial sector became more regulated and received substantial public resources after the crash, doubling its employment share during the 1980s. In 1990, the occupation structure was dominated by nonbusiness services, which represented 48 percent of total employment, while agriculture and manufacturing represented 18 percent each.

The rapid growth of the 1990s once again impacted the labor participation of various economic sectors. The share of agricultural employment fell by almost one-half in this decade, accounting for only 10 percent of total jobs in 2000. The employment shares of mining and manufacturing also declined considerably. The services sector absorbed the decrease in employment in agriculture, mining, and manufacturing, becoming the largest sector by employment, with 67 percent of the workforce. The 1990s saw accelerated GDP growth and a decline in the relative contribution of manufacturing to overall job creation, along with a consolidation of financialization. The first decade and a half of the twenty-first century accentuated the upward trend in the services sector, which reached 70 percent of total employment in 2012, with employment in the agriculture and manufacturing sectors falling to 8 percent and 10 percent, respectively (see Figure 3).

In summary, in this period, we observe even more drastic changes in the distribution of employment than we saw in the productive structure. These are related to the flow of workers from agriculture and manufacturing to the services sector. Within services, the absorption of employment is mainly in

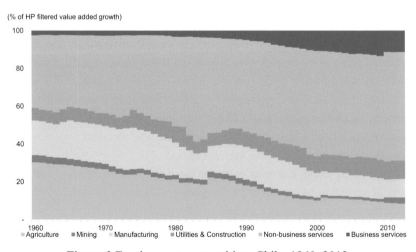

Figure 3 Employment composition, Chile, 1960–2012
(% of employment)

Source: Solimano and Zapata-Román (2022)

the subsectors of commerce, restaurants, and personal and social services. There is a tendency toward financialization, given the high growth of employment in the financial sector. The latter requires more qualified workers and concentrates a greater use of technology than other services, but accounts for only one-quarter of all services, which in turn represent almost 70 percent of total employment in Chile. More recent figures for sectoral GDP indicate that the manufacturing sector continues to shrink, as does the number of jobs, deepening the deindustrialization of the country.

The path followed by the manufacturing sector in Chile is called premature deindustrialization. According to Rodrik (2016), countries experiencing prema-ture deindustrialization observe a sustained decline in both manufacturing value-added and employment shares (secular deindustrialization) before reach-ing the phase of advanced industrialization or even the stage of upgrading industrialization (follow the thicker arrows in Figure 4).

3.2.3 Changes in Labor Productivity

According to McMillan and Rodrik (2011), total labor productivity can grow only for two reasons: first, when productivity rises within a sector through capital accumulation, technological development, or a reduction of plant misallocation; second, when there is reallocation of labor across sectors with different productivity levels, from low-productivity to high-productivity sectors. The first type of prod-uctivity growth is called a "within-sector" component and the second is called "structural change" because it enhances economy-wide productivity growth.

In developing countries, labor productivity gaps are usually very large between sectors. This is particularly the case when these countries have mining enclaves,

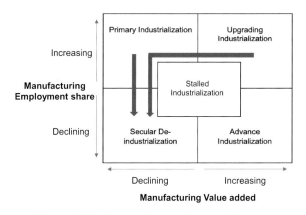

Figure 4 The five varieties of industrialization

Source: Kim and Sumner (2019)

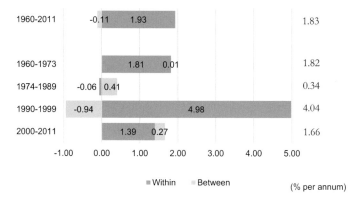

Figure 5 Decomposition of labor productivity growth in Chile, 1960–2011
Note: The decomposition uses the methodology of McMillan and Rodrik (2011).
Source: Solimano and Zapata-Román (2022)

which are technologically intensive but employ a small share of the labor force, as is the case in Africa and Latin America. It was expected that after long dictatorships in the 1980s in many Latin American countries, a new economic environment would yield significantly enhanced productivity performance. However, the intensified competition caused by trade liberalization left fewer manufacturing firms in the market, and displaced workers from closed firms ended up in less-productive activities such as services. Thus the decline in the manufacturing sector translated into growth-reducing structural change.[33]

Chile did not depart from this regional trend. The entire increase in labor productivity from 1960 to 2011 was due to the within-sector component, with a negative structural growth (see Figure 5). The highest productivity increase occurred with the return to democracy in the 1990s, which coincides with a strong economic boost in the country. During this decade, Chile's GDP grew on average 6 percent annually, although the structural change in labor productivity was negative due to the expansion of the services sector in terms of both value added and employment.

Comparing average labor productivity can be misleading if labor shares vary significantly across sectors. For instance, the reason the labor productivity of the mining sector is so high might simply be because the labor share of this highly capital-intensive sector is small. For that reason, we need to analyze together the changes in productivity and changes in employment shares for the different subperiods.

---

[33] McMillan and Rodrik (2011).

We do not observe significant simultaneous rises in relative productivity and employment in any of the periods. The above-average productivity sectors that increase their employment shares from 1960 to 1973 are manufacturing and nonbusiness services; however, the relative productivity in both cases declined in the period. During the dictatorship, relative productivity worsened in most sectors. This was accompanied by escalations in the employment shares of all services, particularly in nonbusiness services. On the contrary, the employment share in manufacturing fell more than four percentage points. In the 1990s, the generation of employment in the services sector was intensified, although at lower levels of relative productivity. The turn of the century came with a slowdown of the economy and minor changes in productivity and employment.

3.2.4 Trade Structure (Exports, Imports)

Another important factor in ST is the diversification of the economy in terms of activities and markets. The Chilean export structure is very constrained in both. Currently, China, the United States, Japan, and South Korea are Chile's main trading partners; together, they receive 57 percent of Chile's total exports.[34]

Copper and its by-products account for almost one-half of total exports; the remaining half is still very concentrated in natural resources, with limited value added. A major weakness of this trade structure is that it makes the country very vulnerable to external shocks. A contraction in demand by any of these four countries, as well as changes in the international prices of the commodities, can affect the entire economy (OECD/UN, 2018).

Despite these weaknesses, there is progress in terms of mineral dependency. From 1962 to 1974, copper and other metals represented on average 87 percent of total exports, a share that was consistently reduced until the beginning of the new century. The boom in copper's price from the 2000s attracted foreign investment in the sector, which again increased the proportion of this metal in total exports. Still the upsurge in the production of other metals, such as lithium, allows some degree of diversification. Besides mining exports, Chile has developed an important agroindustry export sector in winery, fruit, fishmeal, and forestry-related products.

However, Chile's imports map out the limitations of the country's productive structure. From the mid-1980s, on average, 70 percent of the country's imports have been manufactured products. Little progress has been made to revert this tendency, since there has not been a clear decrease in these imports in the past decade. There

---

[34] Simoes and Hidalgo (2011).

has also been a rise in fuel consumption, particularly from the 2000s, directly related to the mining industry, which uses energy-intensive production processes.

3.3 Conclusion

The Chilean development strategy of the past three to four decades has given priority to the acceleration of aggregate economic growth, has relied on orthodox macroeconomic management, and has ensured high profitability for foreign direct investment and big domestic business.[35] There has been a payoff in higher GDP per capita and better living standards, although the benefits of prosperity have been unevenly distributed. To an extent, this prosperity may have been borrowed, as it has relied on the intensive exploitation of nonreproducible natural resources. In addition, from the 2000s, observed rates of GDP growth started to slow down. At the sector level, the economy has specialized in mining, finance, and services, with a diminished share of the manufacturing sector in output that reached a historical low of 10 percent of GDP in 2017.

The empirical analysis of this section shows a decline in the value-added shares of manufacturing and agriculture and a rise in services – particularly finance, trade, and hotels and restaurants – with ups and downs in mining shares in the transition from the ISI strategy to the outward-orientated neoliberal model. These trends are more strongly accentuated for employment shares, with the decline in relative employment generation in agriculture and manufacturing going directly to the services sector, which accounts now for two-thirds of total employment in the economy. Trade liberalization led to severe reductions in the value-added shares of textiles, metal-mechanic, and shoe factories within manufacturing.

A more balanced and sustainable development strategy for Chile, in line with the UNSDGs, for example, would require significant changes in Chile's production structure toward green energy and green production. Policy improvement will require moving away from the intensive use of natural resources and toward knowledge-intensive sectors, a revival of manufacturing, and clean production lines supported by a more environmentally conscious tax system. The reduction of high inequality and deconcentration of wealth, again another recommendation of the UNSDGs, requires important reforms in the tax system and the structure of markets, effective antitrust legislation, and the rebalancing of bargaining capacities between labor and capital that revert the enormous economic surplus currently appropriated by wealthy elites, enabling more inclusive growth.

---

[35] Solimano (2012b).

4 Inflation, Inequality, Growth, and Macroeconomic Management

4.1 Introduction

Macroeconomic policy regimes and macro-financial cycles have shaped the economic development patterns of the Chilean economy for decades. In the ISI period, the Central Bank provided loans to the treasury to finance public sector deficits, and this contributed to chronic inflation. At the same time, distributive conflict between labor and capital over their shares of the national income also contributed to inflation. Private financial markets remained constrained in scope, interest rates were controlled, there were multiple exchange-rate regimes, and capital mobility was controlled. Financial repression of the type characterized by McKinnon (1973) and Shaw (1973) was certainly present in that period, to be followed by full financial deregulation in the second half of the 1970s. During the neoliberal period since the mid 1970s, the prevailing macroeconomic regime has been modified through time. Initially, say right after the military coup, most controlled prices were deregulated in one shot in October 1973, in what was a *first shock treatment*, this time generating a severe jump in inflation of more than 80 percent in one month. A second, *monetarist shock treatment* took place in 1975 to reduce inflation. Then the approach was changed to exchange rate–based disinflation (1979–82), but this policy, along with external shocks, created large current account deficits that were financed with short term capital inflows. In the 1990s and 2000s, macroeconomic policy became more predictable and entailed the adoption of a fiscal rule, inflation targeting, flexible exchange rates, free capital mobility, and Central Bank independence. In this section, we analyze the behavior of inflation, inequality, GDP growth, and macroeconomic management in the period 1940–70 (ISI strategy) and since the mid-1970s in the neoliberal period, suggesting some relevant interactions among these important variables and highlighting features that require further research.

4.2 Inflation

In the nineteenth century, inflation in Chile was low. The 1820s and 1840s were two decades of negative inflation (price deflation). In the following decades, annual inflation fluctuated between 2 and 5 percent (see Table 1). As mentioned in Section 2, Chile had, around the middle of the nineteenth century, a bimetallic monetary system based on gold and silver with full currency convertibility that was abandoned in years of financial distress and war. For a few decades, money was issued by commercial banks but then toward the century there was the

Table 1 Chilean inflation rate by decade, 1811–2017 (percentage of variation in the Consumer Price Index by decade and average annual variation rate)

Period	Percentage	Average annual variation	Period	Percentage	Average annual variation
1811–20	22	2	1920–30	30	3
1820–30	−21	−3	1930–40	94	7
1830–40	5	0	1940–50	412	18
1840–50	23	−2	1950–60	2089	36
1850–60	34	3	1960–70	1028	26
1860–70	0	1	1970–80	437006	162
1870–80	62	5	1980–90	529	21
1880–90	57	5	1990–2000	124	10
1890–1900	58	5	2000–10	36	3
1900–10	109	8	2010–17	25	3
1910–20	74	6			

Source: Own elaboration based on official statistics and Lüders and colleagues (2016)

emergence of fiscal money. The country also adhered to the gold standard between 1895 and 1898, but this was short-lived. In the first decades of the twentieth century, there was an upward trend in inflation in the one-digit range. Inflationary pressures mounted in the decades after the Great Depression, with inflation reaching close to 20 percent annually in the 1940s, 36 percent in the 1950s, and 26 percent in the 1960s. The 1970s was the decade of highest inflation recorded in the twentieth century, averaging at 162 percent per year to decline, gradually, to 20 percent in the 1980s, 10 percent in the 1990s, and around 3 percent in the first two decades of the twenty-first century (see Table 1).

Figure 6 depicts the record of inflation between 1811 and 2017, showing decade averages. The highest inflation period was from the 1940s to the 1970s. The three governments of the centrist Radical Party, spanning 1938 to 1952 (with Presidents Pedro Aguirre Cerda, Juan Antonio Rios, and Gabriel Gonzalez Videla) were associated with a tide toward higher inflation that escalated rapidly during the Ibañez government (1952–8). Ibañez tried orthodox (IMF-style) stabilization to control inflation without much success. Then Jorge Alessandri Rodriguez's government (1958–64) adopted exchange rate–based stabilization of inflation during the early part of its mandate and continued with a more eclectic approach. Eduardo Frei Montalva's government (1964–70) combined demand management and exchange rate management to reduce inflation combining cost-based with

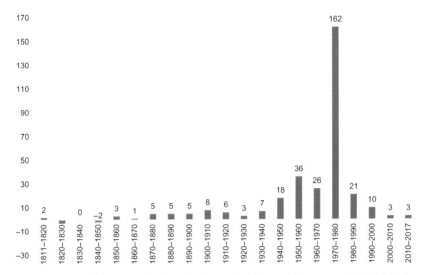

Figure 6 Inflation rate by decade since the nineteenth century, 1811–2017
(average annual variation in the Consumer Price Index, percent)

Source: Own elaboration based on official statistics and Lüders et al. (2016)

demand policies (see Figure 7).[36] It was not easy for policymakers to control inflation in that period.

The rise in inflation in the 1940s and 1950s was associated with the monetization of fiscal deficits on the demand side and a greater role of organized labor since the 1950s represented by the Central Unica de Trabajadores (CUT), led by Clotario Blest, a charismatic labor leader with a background in Christian-anarchist ideas. Workers pushed for a shift in functional income distribution in their favor given their gained strength and political influence. The labor movement, until the military coup of September 1973, showed a capacity to resist the erosion of real wages due to inflation but faced the hostility of certain governments, particularly that of former general Ibañez, who always showed an anti-labor proclivity and wanted to make wage earners absorb most of the cost of stabilizing inflation. A few decades later, another army general, Pinochet, would adopt the same recipe of making labor to pay the cost of stopping inflation.

Ibañez's policies led to social and political destabilization with the most dramatic episode being the "Battle of Santiago" of April 2–3, 1957, when widespread riots erupted in response to rises in public transport fares decreed by the government. To control the social uprising, Ibañez first brought the Carabineros (national

---

[36] We can distinguish three main approaches to inflation: monetarist, cost push, and distributive conflict.

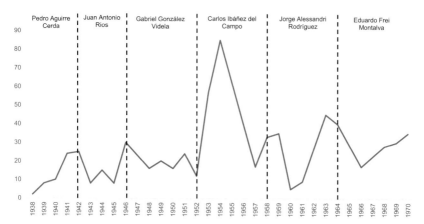

Figure 7 Inflation rate in the period 1938–1970 (average annual variation in the Consumer Price Index, percent)

Source: Own elaboration based on official statistics and Lüders and colleagues (2016)

police) and then the army, which occupied Santiago, killing a score of demonstrators.[37]

Inflation continued in the 1960s during the reformist government of Frei Montalva (1964–70), although the government tried to stabilize it through a coordinated management of wages, the exchange rate, the money supply, and the price of public utilities. In 1971, the Allende government decreed generous wage increases and expanded fiscal spending, and inflation accelerated in 1972 and 1973. There were food shortages, price controls, and the hoarding of essential goods by households with high liquidity. The UP government gave priority to rapid redistribution of income to the urban working class and peasants, while running large fiscal deficits covered by money printing. However, due to the blockade of foreign loans to the Allende government induced by the Nixon administration, it also faced a severe foreign exchange constraint that prevented an adequate level of imports of critical goods (food, capital goods, inputs), reducing existing supplies in the market. Foreign loans by international financial organizations and private banks were cut under pressures from the Nixon administration as a response to the policies of copper nationalization adopted by the Allende government and supported by the full political spectrum in the Chilean congress.

A few weeks after the military coup of September 1973, controlled prices of basic foodstuffs were deregulated and public tariffs of transport and utilities

---

[37] For an account of "transport riots" and "food riots" in Chile and other countries, see chapter 4 in Solimano (2022).

were adjusted upward very sharply, depressing real wages. This could be considered the first episode of economic shock treatment the military junta undertook after seizing power. These sharp adjustments in administered prices led to a *jump in the price level of 87 percent in October 1973*. This was a severe price shock, concentrated in one month and decreed by the military government, that severely depressed real wages and real balances and had lasting consequences for living standards and economic activity for the working class.

The stabilization of inflation proved to be a slow process in subsequent years. Monthly inflation rates remained in the vicinity of 10 percent between 1974 and 1976, despite the military junta's application of a monetarist shock treatment in 1975 to abate inflation. Inertial/sticky inflation disconcerted the Chicago Boys trained in the neoclassical doctrine of market-clearing prices and downward flexibility of the price level. They could not understand that after a sharp, policy-induced decline in aggregate demand, prices could continue to increase.

In view of the persistence in inflation, the military government, besides keeping the rate of unemployment high to discipline workers so they would moderate their wage demands, slowed the rate of devaluation of the exchange rate (peso to dollar) to reduce the cost pressures coming from the local cost of imported goods; apparently the policymakers started to use a theory of cost-based inflation rather than a pure monetary-quantity theory approach to reduce inflation. It is worth noting that at that time, the Central Bank, an important player in reducing inflation, was not independent of the government. The military junta approved the Central Bank's independence only in October 1989, a few months before the scheduled departure of the military regime. This legislation has been in place for more than three decades in democracy.

The approach of slowing exchange rate adjustments was also aimed to reduce *expectations* of future inflation. It is an empirical regularity that in an open economy subject to high price uncertainty – Chile in the mid-1970s – economic agents tend to use the exchange rate as a predictor of future inflation.

Disinflation in the 1980s and 1990s was only gradual. Consumer Price Index inflation was 27.3 percent in 1990 (its highest peak since the onset of the 1981 recession), but by 2006, it had fallen to less than 3 percent. The next year, however, in 2007, it had accelerated to 7.8 percent and in 2008, it was 7.1 percent in the wake of several food and energy price increases. In the recession year of 2009, inflation turned *negative* to −1.4 percent, the first year of deflation in more than seven decades in Chile (see Figure 8).

The post-Pinochet governments wanted to establish their credibility as guardians of price stability and sound macroeconomic management to attract foreign capital and encourage domestic private investment. A distancing to left-wing policies under Allende of fiscal expansion, generous wage increases, and

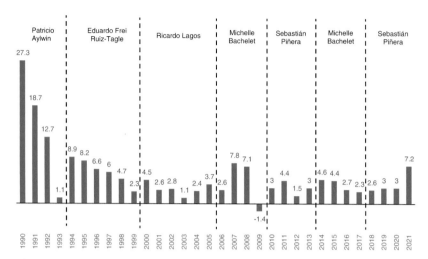

Figure 8 Annual inflation rate by presidential periods in democracy, 1990–2021
(average variation in the Consumer Price Index, percent)

Source: Own elaboration based on data from Banco Central (2022)

monetary expansion was sought by the reconstructed Chilean left. Fiscal deficits were maintained at a low level and labor legislation was timidly reformed in some respects, but, overall, the labor code of the Pinochet regime, which prevented labor unions from negotiating at the level of industrial branches, was maintained. The notion of labor market flexibility – low costs of firing workers – was held as the mantra in labor relations. All these factors helped the convergence of inflation to the one-digit level by avoiding the wage pushes that provoked so many headaches for policymakers in the 1950s and 1960s, decades of much stronger labor unions.

There is a controversy about the extent to which the shift to lower inflation worldwide (Chile included) since the 1990s until the 2021/2 post-COVID resumption of inflation has been due to more zealous monetary authorities with little tolerance for inflation following a mandate for many central banks to care "only" on controlling inflation (a monetarist view). An alternative view (cost-based) of disinflation in the period 1990–2020 is that the decline in wage and inflationary pressures (before 2020) has been associated mainly with the deflationary shock of the incorporation of more than 1 billion new workers to the world economy – producing manufacturing oriented to international trade – in China, India, and the former Soviet Union.[38] The legal mandate for the

---

[38] Counteracting these anti-inflationary external trends is the increase in oil and food prices accelerating in 2008 and then again in 2010 and in 2021–2.

Chilean Central Bank was maintaining low and stable inflation and ensuring the normalcy of internal and external payments of the Chilean economy. Full employment is *not* an explicit objective of the Central Bank.

In the 2000s, the socialist government of Ricardo Lagos followed a macroeconomic policy mix that could be considered orthodox in line with the latest fashions in international macroeconomics and IMF recommendations prevailing at that time. Managed exchange rates were abandoned in favor of free floating and taxes on short-term capital inflows were eliminated. An important piece in the whole package was the introduction of a *structural fiscal surplus budget rule (SB)* that is considered a Chilean innovation in this area.

The fiscal rule was intended to operate as a self-imposed policy of fiscal restraint to shield the government from eventual pressures to increase public spending coming from politicians, social organizations, and even representatives of big capital. The analytic idea behind the structural fiscal rule is on the surface simple but not without problems of implementation: fiscal spending should follow long-run (permanent) values of the price of copper and GDP growth, the two key parameters affecting the revenues side of the budget. These two variables are not easy to predict with accuracy.

The first Bachelet government, within the framework of the Fiscal Responsibility Act, created an economic and social stabilization fund that replaced the existing copper stabilization fund and created a pension reserve fund operated by the state.[39] Central Bank independence was consolidated and inflation targeting – guided by the "Taylor rule" in which interest rates are adjusted to correct deviations of inflation from the target set by the Central Bank besides deviations of output from full capacity – became the model for conducting monetary policy. This policy framework for monetary policy has remained in place.

4.3 Inequality

A structural feature of the Chilean economy and society is high and persistent inequality. The historical roots of inequality come from the colonial period and the concentrated ownership of productive land and mineral resources in the hands of *peninsulares* and *criollos*. Independence in the nineteenth century from the Spanish crown did *not* reduce economic inequality in significant ways. It basically shifted part of the property of productive wealth from the Spanish to a national economic elite of landowners, traders, and industry producers. British entrepreneurs and financiers in the nineteenth century took an important

---

[39] The SB rule improved its methodology of income measurement and in 2011, under the first administration of President Sebastián Piñera, a second-generation methodology was applied, giving rise to the cyclically adjusted (fiscal) balance (CA). In addition, an advisory fiscal council was set up in 2013 to monitor enforcement of the rule.

role as owners of nitrate, railways, and banking. American multinational corporations in the twentieth century played an important role in the copper sector.

The existing political system in Chile, supported by the constitutions of 1833 and 1980 and the sheer power of economic elites, landowners, economic conglomerates, and financial oligarchies, has made it very difficult to undertake durable redistributive policies that could alter, in a structural way, income and wealth distribution to a more egalitarian distribution. Predictably, inequality became chronically entrenched, with high Gini coefficients prevailing for a period of more than 150 years. The Gini index experiences some variations through time but remains persistently in the range of 50 to 60 percent, which is rather high by international standards.

An attempt to reduce endemic income inequality took place in the period 1938–73 of ISI. This period included the Popular Front governments of the late 1930s and early 1940s and then other centrist administrations.

Historically, the share of the top 1 percent in income has varied from 28 percent in 1938 to near 18 percent in 1952 (the period of the Radical Party governments and the first decade and a half of ISI industrialization). However, during the government of Ibañez, the income share of the top 1 percent was almost *restored to its 1938 level*. This was a period of acceleration of inflation with stabilization attempts based on wage contention and orthodox fiscal and monetary policies. Then, in the first three years of the Alessandri Rodriguez government, the top 1 percent share declined, coinciding with the decline in inflation in those years. The share also declined at the start of the Frei Montalva government (Rodriguez Weber, 2014).

The Gini coefficient declined during the Allende government, particularly in 1971, reaching its lowest historical level, but high inflation started in 1972 that affected the purchasing power of salaries and wages. The Gini coefficient increased substantially during the Pinochet regime (a period of higher inequality), coinciding with macroeconomic shock treatment, deregulation, privatization, repression of labor unions, and external financial integration. Then came a decline in inequality in the civilian governments after Pinochet, stabilizing, however, in levels only below 50 percent.

4.4 The Ups and Downs of Economic Growth

From 1940 to 1985, Chilean economic growth was not spectacular. It fluctuated with the evolution of terms of trade, the adoption of anti-inflationary policies, the size of the internal market, the dynamism of the international economy, the growth of productivity, and the sociopolitical cycles of social peace and social conflict that affected private investment and government policies.

The average rate of growth of GDP in the period 1940–85 was 3.1 percent while GDP grew in 1986–2009 by an average of nearly 5.4 percent. In the second half of the 1980s, the growth rate started to accelerate in comparison with its historical record of the 1940–85 period (see Figures 9 and 10). A factor that contributed to the growth recovery of the second half of the 1980s after the deep economic and financial crises of 1982–3 was that the economy had significant unused productive capacities after a major economic contraction in 1982–3 in which GDP fell by an accumulated 16 percent.

Nonetheless, that growth acceleration was not permanent (see Figure 10). The golden growth years were between 1986 and 1998, in which it averaged

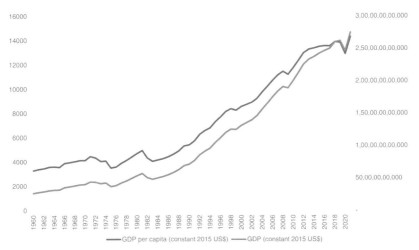

Figure 9 Chile: Total and per capita GDP (constant 2015 US$)

Source: Own elaboration based on data from World Bank (2022a)

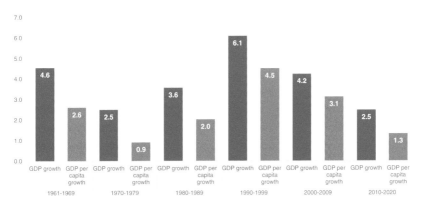

Figure 10 Total and per capita GDP growth rate (%), by decade

Source: Own elaboration based on data from World Bank (2022a)

Figure 11 Chile: Growth swings and crisis, 1961–2021, GDP growth (annual %)
Source: Own elaboration based on data from World Bank (2022b)

7.3 percent per year. Then came the East Asian crisis and a recession in 1999 with growth in the 2000–9 period reduced to an annual average of 3.7 percent. In turn, GDP growth further decelerated to an annual average growth rate of 2.5 percent between 2010 and 2020. Figure 10 shows GDP and GDP per capita growth rates by decades from 1960 to 2020, highlighting that the best growth decade of the past six decades was the 1990s followed by the 2000s. Thereafter, apparently, the engines of growth of the neoliberal period based on exports (in an extractive modality of obtaining rents from national resources) along with an expansion of the services sector and financial activities were running out of steam.

The growth record of the past six decades has been volatile and bumpy, as shown in Figure 11, punctuated by two, largely homemade big recessions in 1975 (shock treatment) and 1982–3 (twin currency and banking crises after financial deregulation) and two milder recessions in 1998 and 2009 associated with the Asian and Russian crises in the late 1990s and the financial crisis of the late 2000s in the United States and Europe, respectively, and a medium-sized recession in 2020 associated with the COVID pandemic.

The acceleration in economic growth in the 1990s and 2000s compared with the historical record of the period 1940–85 has been often attributed to two broad factors underlying the "policy climate" of Chile's post-Pinochet democracy. This period was, apparently, one of social peace and "domestic consensus" between various center–left governments and right-wing opposition around the maintenance of the neoliberal model in a low-intensity democracy: this provided guarantees to the business community to ensure a level of private investment that delivered respectable economic growth.

The first two decades after the departure of the military regime saw a largely "dormant" civil society and a marginalized labor movement traumatized by seventeen years of military rule accompanied by regressive economic policies and repressive politics. As democracy gradually consolidated, society started to wake up with a series of student movement irruptions in 2006 and 2011 accompanied by environmental and feminist activism in the second decade of the twenty-first century, culminating with a peak of social unrest – the *estallido social* – in October and November 2019.

From an economic perspective, neoliberalism played out the profit motive as an engine to stimulate capital accumulation and growth. In turn, the *profit-led growth regime* was helped by a demobilized labor movement that enabled a supply of "well-behaved," relatively inexpensive labor power to the private productive sector of the economy (the capitalist sector), ensuring good profits.[40] However, the booming investment and growth period did not extend beyond the first decade of the twenty-first century as there was a marked tendency for economic growth to stall.

In retrospect, the neoliberal reform that began in the mid-1970s under Pinochet translated into a growth boom that was observed more fully in the 1990s – that is, ten to fifteen years *after* the neoliberal policies of macroeconomic stabilization, external opening, privatization, and liberalization of financial markets were initially launched. By the 1990s, the neoliberal policies were already complemented by the restoration of democracy, giving a degree of domestic and international legitimacy to the Chilean economic model, particularly in financial circles and mainstream public opinion. However, the neoliberal system also incubated its own *internal contradictions*. Inequality and environmental degradation are two main contradictions in the road to sustained growth. Higher inequality is shown in persistent gaps in income and wealth levels among the upper and lower segments of society; further, the compression of the labor share in national income largely excluded labor from a fair share in economic prosperity. Pro-capital, profit-led growth was the norm, with labor subordinated. The other side of the coin of the relentless pursue of profits in an extractive economy relying on mining and natural resource extraction was *environmental degradation* affecting growth performance.

The orthodox view of the golden age of high growth is predicated on the basis that Chile had strong "macroeconomic fundamentals" (low inflation, absence of fiscal and external imbalances, financial stability). However, the macro approach neglects the potential role of industrial policy and, contrarily, the consequences of dispensing with it altogether. Unfortunately, the dominant approach of different administrations over the past three decades was that industrial policy was either unnecessary or, worse, unproductive. This is an

---

[40] See Solimano and Gutierrez (2008).

oversimplistic view: Chile spends a very low percentage on research and development (R&D) – no more than 0.5 percent of GDP versus 2.5 percent in OECD countries – and as a consequence it experiences low productivity growth, impairing long-run GDP growth.

The overwhelming focus on macroeconomic conditions resonated well in the Chilean case. In fact, the country suffered the trauma of the inflationary crises of the 1970s and currency devaluation and financial collapse in the early 1980s that interrupted economic growth and caused a huge surge in unemployment, a decline in real wages, and deterioration in human welfare. The economic crisis of the early 1980s was followed by four years (1983–7) of social unrest, mass demonstrations, violence, and repression that eventually forced the Pinochet regime to negotiate a return to democracy. In turn, the post-Pinochet governments, both center–left and right-wing administrations, have given central priority to macroeconomic management and maintaining private-sector-led economic growth over the reduction of inequality and the meeting of environmental goals.

Chile anticipated the orthodoxy of the times regarding macroeconomic management. In the late 1980s, at the end of the Pinochet regime, and with the apparent agreement of the political center–left opposition of the time, Chile established the independent Central Bank with the mandate of ensuring low and stable inflation and normalcy in internal and external payments.[41] Steady GDP growth, full employment, and the maintenance of an "adequate" (equilibrium) stable exchange rate are *not included* as explicit policy objectives, according to the constitutional charter of the Chilean Central Bank. This is certainly different from the objectives of the central banks of several advanced economies, most notably the US Federal Reserve. However, over time, inflation became the policy objective of several central banks both in some advanced countries and in emerging economies.[42] In turn, the independent Central Bank of Chile as guardian of monetary stability was to be shielded from political pressures.[43] The president and board of directors of the bank are appointed for ten years and form a small elite of public officials enjoying super-stable and well-paid jobs in which they make important decisions (with various distributive effects) that affect the course of the economy and the welfare of various economic agents.

---

[41] See Blanchard and colleagues (2010) and Solimano (2010) for reassessments of the macroeconomic orthodoxy of the 1990s and 200s regarding Central Bank policy and fiscal policy in light of the financial crisis of 2007–9 in advanced economies.

[42] Of course, monetary authorities cannot be completely oblivious to the real cycles of the economy, nor to the effects of their own policies on the intensity and timing of these cycles. In Chile, Central Bank authorities must report to the congress each year on the state of the economy.

[43] Albeit no need was seen to insulate the bank from the influence coming from the powerful commercial bank community and other financial operators always sensitive to the interest rate and exchange rate decisions of the monetary authorities.

4.5 Resource and Environmental Sustainability of Chilean Growth

An important question is the extent to which economic growth is sustainable over time. An influential sustainability criterion was provided by Sir John Hicks, a famous British economist, who maintained that *sustainable real income* (and thus sustainable growth trajectories) is one in which future generations are not impaired by the savings and investment decisions made in the present that affect future growth. This concept is relevant to evaluating the sustainability of Chilean growth, particularly given its excessive reliance on natural resources (renewable and nonrenewable), its high-intensity energy use, its high geographical and proprietary concentration of productive assets, and the environmental implications of its export base. Critical questions that must be addressed by any current and future government are the following.

4.5.1 Can Natural Resources Use Continue to Be Sustained As an Export Base?

It is estimated that around 70 percent of Chilean exports (more than 35 percent of GDP) rely on raw materials and processed natural resources: copper, fruits, fishmeal, timber, and others. For a country that follows an extractive growth pattern, the pressures on natural resources and the environment are very significant.[44]

4.5.2 Can Energy-Intensive Growth Be Sustained?

In the early 2000s, a joint evaluation carried out by the OECD with the United Nations Economic Commission for Latin America and the Caribbean (UN-ECLAC) on the environmental and energy consequences of rapid growth in Chile warned about the intensity of Chilean energy consumption (the GDP growth-energy elasticity was above unity) (CEPAL and OCDE, 2005). Nowadays, expert analysts still warn about the enormous need to generate adequate electricity supplies and the use of water resources in the copper sector and in the fruit industry, two key sectors of Chilean exports. Of course, how this electricity is generated is critical for the environment and the quality of life of populations living in areas close to energy-generation plants. According to Chile's National Energy Commission (see Figures 12 and 13), in 2021, the main sources of electricity generation were coal and natural gas followed by hydroelectric sources. In contrast, in most of the 2000s, the main source of electricity generation was hydroelectric. The share of wind-based electricity, solar power, and other renewable generation is still low, but has grown rapidly in the past five years. It is striking that changing the energy matrix

---

[44] Sunkel (1994) provides an early analysis of the pressure of rapid growth on water resources, energy, forestry, and the environment in Chile.

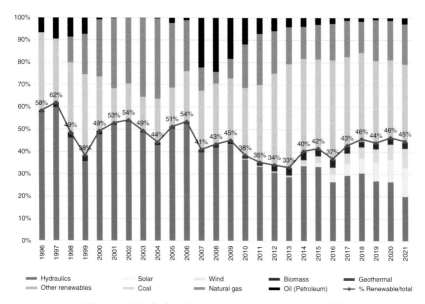

Figure 12 Relative share by generation source (%)

Source: Own elaboration based on data from Generadoras de Chile (2022)

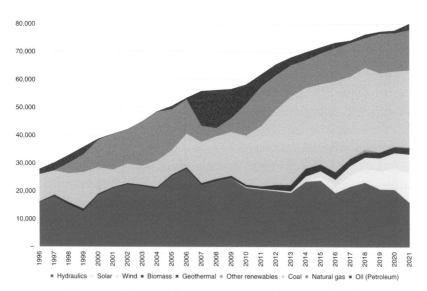

Figure 13 Volume of energy generated by source (GWh)

Source: Own elaboration based on data from Generadoras de Chile (2022)

toward more environmentally friendly energy sources was not prioritized earlier. This is a surprising feature for a country with more than 3,000 coasts and the world's driest desert, such as Chile.

4.5.3 Can the Environment Continue to Withstand Rapid Growth?

The consequences of rapid growth on the environment are quite serious. Resources devoted to prevention and mitigation of the environmental consequences of economic growth are still limited. Rapid growth in GDP and consumption has a variety of direct effects on the environment – an increase in fossil fuel emissions and other pollutants; an intensive use of energy to meet consumption demands; the overexploitation of water, soil, and forestry resources; the rapid extraction of sea products and aggressive mining extraction; and congestion in urban areas associated with a sharp increase in the stock of cars and transport vehicles.

4.5.4 Challenges for Structural Transformation

Important challenges remain on the real side of the economy such as sustainability of growth, diversification of the country's economic structure, faster productivity growth, and ecological protection. As the country approaches higher levels of per capita income, convergence to the high growth rates of the mid-1980s and 1990s (6–7 percent per year) is highly unlikely. Further acceleration in the rate of economic growth will depend more on productivity growth and technical improvements than on factor accumulation because of diminishing returns to capital. In addition, natural resources will be severely strained with an attempt to achieve higher growth based on the consumption of natural capital that the current practice follows. In turn, there is the current *composition* of growth, as discussed in Section 3. Trends in ST are tilted to mining and services, with a diminished manufacturing sector. A reversal of these trends may not be easy; currently, Chile spends less than 0.4 percent of its GDP on R&D (well below the average OECD level of around 2.5 percent of GDP), and successive governments have been reluctant to adopt more active industrial policies. Also, the value-added intensity of the export bundle remains moderate, as the country still relies on the export of commodities (copper) with relatively low value added, although agroindustry exports are more labor-intensive. In the most recent OECD Productive Transformation Policy Review, the need for an update of Chile's development strategy was highlighted. The review stresses the importance of increasing factor productivity growth, lowering the territorial concentration of production, raising value addition in services, and reducing overreliance on mining, among other deficiencies. The report proposed exploiting opportunities in green production, developing solar energy, increasing digitalization, and investing in big data and broader internet connections. The emphasis and recommendations of the report seem reasonable, although it is probably overoptimistic in its assessment of the willingness and ability of governments, inspired by a hands-off approach to development, to carry out this update of the Chilean development strategy (OECD/UN, 2018).

4.6 Concluding Remarks

Chilean economic performance has been historically characterized by fluctuating growth, chronic inflation (particularly in the 1940–80 period), and persistent inequality. Chronic inflation prevailed from the 1940s to the 1980s (the 1970s was the most inflationary decade), although it eventually converged to international inflation in the early decades of the twenty-first century. Programs of economic stabilization in the mid-1950s (General Ibañez) and the mid-1970s (General Pinochet) were orthodox and based on demand shocks and wage compression. Exchange rate–based stabilization was tried in the late 1950s, early 1960s, late 1970s, and early 1980s. Mainstream institutional innovation took place in the 1990s and 2000s, comprising Central Bank independence, inflation targeting, fiscal rules, flexible exchange rates, and sovereign wealth funds.

The neoliberal revolution led by the Pinochet regime in the 1970s and 1980s brought severe social costs, slow disinflation, and bubble-led growth combined with episodes of recession and financial crises. Inequality of income remained high and wealth concentration reached record levels. In the 1990s, with the restoration of democracy, there was a continuity in the neoliberal economic model, but it was tempered by higher social spending, more public investment, and reforms in the social sectors.

Inequality has been a chronic problem in Chilean society since colonial rule; this feature was not reversed during the independence process in the nineteenth century. In the twentieth century, inequality declined somewhat in the period 1940–73 but increased sharply with the neoliberal policies adopted during the Pinochet regime. Income inequality started to decline after the return of democracy although wealth inequality remains very high. The historical record of the 1950s and 1970s shows that a rise in inflation increased personal income inequality (Gini coefficients) concentrated incomes at the top and reduced labor shares in national income.

In this section, we have documented the turning point in the growth dynamics of the Chilean economy in the mid-to-late 1980s when the country started to accelerate its historical rate of growth of GDP, particularly in the period 1986–98. The growth process of the prior four to five decades was not smooth, particularly in the 1970s and 1980s. Big recessions occurred in 1975 and 1982–3 with more moderate recessions taking place in 1999 and 2009 and a significant recession in 2020 led by the COVID pandemic. After nearly a quarter century of growth acceleration, albeit accompanied by volatility, economic growth decelerated in the post-2009 period, affected by slower productivity growth, the gradual loss of dynamism of leading sectors, and the emergence of social unrest in a country of persistent inequalities and environmental fragility.

5 Social Policies, Poverty, and Inequality

5.1 Introduction

Social protection and social policies that provide education, healthcare, and pensions, among other benefits, are the primary tools states use to reduce poverty and inequality, manage social risks, and boost shared prosperity among their citizens. These types of policies also seek to protect individuals against shocks and contingencies related to macro disturbances (recessions, financial crisis), risks in the job market (layoffs, unemployment, cuts in wages) and the life cycle (death and injuries), thus helping them protect their human capital. Promoting investment in human capital (education and health) helps individuals in enhancing opportunities to access productive work to improve their economic possibilities and earning capacities.[45]

In this section, we analyze the effects of the main economic and social neoliberal reforms and policies implemented in Chile in the past fifty years on poverty and inequality and the provision of social services. These policies had profound effects on the labor market (employment and salaries), as well as on the provision of social protection in often regressive ways. Neoliberal economic reforms applied over several decades dramatically affected the country's productive structure, its growth potential, and even its cultural attitudes toward solidarity, competition, and the social tolerance of the profit motive.[46]

Social reforms implemented since the 1980s that allowed the private provision of social services such as healthcare, education, pensions, and social housing were promoted to improve efficiency in the markets and increase individual choice. At the same time, the military regime passed new laws that allowed for-profit providers to operate in the education, healthcare, housing, and pension-fund management sectors. These commercial providers could start charging fees at "market prices" for social services.

Pricing was not the only critical dimension. Given the complex nature of education and healthcare services, along with the fact that the privatized social security system was based on risk–return combinations hardly understood by the population, issues of highly imperfect and asymmetric information and insufficient regulation under oligopolistic market structures also became very relevant.

---

[45] Barrientos (2012); World Bank (2022a).
[46] Ffrench-Davis (2018); Jadresic (1986); Solimano (2012b).

Although more regulation and expansion of social services were introduced after the return of democracy in the 1990s, the overall market orientation of social policies undertaken in the Pinochet era was largely preserved afterward.

Market-orientated social policies shifted the cost of accessing social services to beneficiaries, reducing state financial burden, and increasing it for households. Predictably, this contributed to widen the segmentation and profound inequalities in access to quality services, creating dual markets in which the quality of the service is positively correlated with the family's incomes purchasing power and financial capacity.

The first part of this section analyses the role of the state in reducing poverty and inequality from the 1990s to the present. It first analyses the evolution of poverty, the main drivers behind the important reduction experienced in this area, and the main social policies that contributed to its reduction. We then analyze income distribution and the evolution of wealth inequality, which, unlike the case of poverty, has remained very unequal since the return to democracy, underscoring the limited role of the Chilean state in enabling progressive changes in overall inequality. The second part of the section describes the main (neoliberal) reforms and policies carried out in education, healthcare, pensions, and the labor market during the dictatorship period to the present.

5.2 Income Poverty

The return to democracy after 1990 was a period of rising private investment and job creation that helped reverse the rise in unemployment and the depression of real wages of the dictatorship period, with average GDP growth rates of more than 7 percent between 1991 and 1998.[47] The rapid growth of this decade and following ones moved Chile from having a GDP per capita in a low rank in South America (PPP current international prices), $4,504, in 1990 to taking the lead in the region from 2010, reaching $29,104 in 2021 (World Bank, 2022a).

High growth had a positive effect on the reduction of the poverty head count, which decreased more than eighteen percentage points during the 1990s, from 38.6 percent in 1990 to 20.2 percent in 2000 (old methodology) – or from 68.5 percent to 37.5 percent using the new methodology to measure head count poverty.[48] After 2000, as shown in Figure 14, the poverty rate reduced further, reaching 8.5 percent in 2017 (MDSF and PNUD, 2020). But poverty increased

---

[47] Contreras and Ffrench-Davis (2012).

[48] In 2013, three main methodological changes were made to how the country measured head count poverty. First, there was an adjustment in the poverty line. Second, there was a change in the estimation of a per capita poverty line for a poverty line per equivalent person. Finally, the new methodology changed the household welfare indicator, replacing the total per capita household income with the household income per equivalent person.

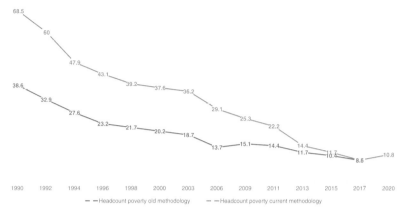

Figure 14 Evolution of poverty, 1990–2020 (head count, percent; old and current methodology)

Source: Own elaboration, data from MDSF and PNUD (2020)

again during the COVID pandemic in 2020 to 10.8 percent. These absolute measures of poverty use a threshold defined as the minimum income necessary to satisfy food and nonfood needs. When using a relative threshold, such as 50 percent of the median household income, OECD data show a higher poverty rate, which has only fallen from 17.8 percent in 2009 to 16 .5 percent in 2017 (OECD, 2018b).

An increase in social spending since 2006 and the creation of a social protection system called Chile Solidario in 2004 under the Lagos government played a key role in overcoming extreme poverty. The program helped families and people living in extreme poverty enter social protection networks and access better living conditions. Its main components were psychosocial support, preferential access to social services, and guaranteed access to subsidies, including cash transfers. In 2013, the program was replaced by the Security and Opportunities (Seguridades y Oportunidades) program, also known as Ethical Family Income, which benefits vulnerable and poor households (with incomes under the poverty line or just above).

One of the key features of the social protection system is the capacity to identify the poorest 40–60 percent of the population to be reached through targeted social programs. The targeting process improved considerably with the creation of the social protection card (*ficha de protección social*) in 2006. This tool identified lower-income families, via household surveys, to be beneficiaries of cash transfers. To move toward a more efficient allocation of monetary transfers, excluding only the higher-income families, in 2016, the social protection card was replaced by the households social registry (*registro social de hogares*). The main innovation of this registry is that it stopped relying on self-reported instruments as a primary source of information to carry out the socioeconomic classification of households, replacing it with administrative records from different public services such as the Internal Revenue Service, the Home Office (Ministry of the Interior), the Institute of Social Security (IPS, by its Spanish acronym), the Health Superintendence, and the Ministry of Education, among others. Since its creation, the social registry has almost doubled the number of registered households, with information on 84.4 percent of the population in August 2021 (MDSF, 2022).

Due to the existence of fiscal budget constraints, targeted social programs have been a common practice not only in Chile, but also in Latin America. However, as the country has moved toward higher levels of income and significant poverty reduction, the discussion has turned toward the universalization of social benefits as in a welfare state. Under universalism, the whole population – or a specific group in the case of sectorial policies – receives social benefits that are considered basic rights, while only a part of the population is selected to receive social benefits. The questioning of targeting arises in determining who deserves and gets the benefits, a discussion that raises operational and normative issues. The registry system that allows accurate targeting is expensive to update, and changes to people's incomes are usually faster than adjustments in administrative records, especially those of lower-income families who usually have informal jobs and face costs to reach the registries. This might lead to a suboptimal allocation of public resources (too little social spending) aimed at poverty reduction.

On the other hand, targeting can generate perverse incentives to underreport income to appear poorer than reality to obtain the benefits. It can also directly discourage work to avoid exceeding the income threshold set to qualify for social programs. There is also a potentially psychologic harmful effect of targeted programs on self-esteem and self-respect, implicit in asking for help from the state and in having to prove that one needs public help. Politicians can also use targeted aid to maintain a system of patronage over a particular population. Finally, maintaining targeted social program could discourage the state sector from increasing social spending.[49]

Thus citizen demands have gone in the direction of universalizing social policies, which poses both operational and budgetary challenges for the state. The progressive universalization by which social benefits are delivered to an increasing population requires a precise identification system and permanent updating. The COVID-19 pandemic accelerated this process in Chile since the instruments used (such as income transfers to households) were targeted to the 80 percent most vulnerable listed in the social registry of households – increasing the incentives to be in this registry. On the budget side, increasing social spending

---

[49] Held and Kaya (2007); Mkandawire (2007); Solimano (2022).

requires rising tax revenue, which is currently well below the average of the OECD; this will be further discussed in the following subsections.

5.2.1 Income and Wealth Inequality

There is extensive evidence that Chile is a highly unequal country compared to other nations. If we focus on income inequality, Chile is almost at the top of the list in inequality among OECD countries (after Costa Rica in 2021). Further, it ranks among the top ten countries with the highest inequality in the world (World Bank, 2020). Although the Gini coefficient (close to 0.5) shows a decline in inequality from the year 2000, this decreasing trend has largely stopped from 2010, as shown in Figure 15, which depicts the evolution of the Gini coefficient since 1990 for different types of income. The difference between the Gini coefficient of autonomous income and the Gini coefficient of monetary income corresponds to the redistribution carried out by the state (transfers and subsidies). Both measures follow the same trajectory with very small differences, suggesting that tax redistribution is very limited in the country – although it has increased since 2009 (we will discuss this point later in the section).

From 2000 to 2015, the Gini coefficient fell by almost six points due to an increase in real average wages, upgrading in the minimum wage, and cash transfers to the poor. During these years, the income of the poorest decile grew 145 percent in real terms, while that of the upper decile grew 30 percent. However, in absolute terms, while the most deprived decile increased its income by two and a half times, that of the upper 10 percent grew ninefold. It is not surprising, then, that although the disadvantaged populations more than doubled their real earnings, their perception of a significant income gap with more affluent groups persists (PNUD, 2017).

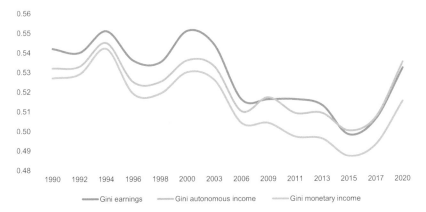

Figure 15 Gini index for different income sources

Source: Own elaboration, data from MDSF (2021) and MDSF and PNUD (2020)

Not only is the flow income unevenly distributed, but also the stock of personal wealth (financial and nonfinancial) is very concentrated at the top. Each year, the Credit Suisse Research Institute produces an international report including people with more than $1 million in liquid wealth (high net worth) and those with more than $50 million (ultra-high net wealth). Including these "rich and super-rich people" in the analysis, the Gini coefficient of wealth in Chile reached 0.79 in 2017, much higher than the Gini coefficient of (monetary) income of 0.49 for that same year.[50]

A much higher indicator of wealth inequality in Chile is estimated by the World Inequality Database (WID, 2022) of the Paris School of Economics World Economic Lab, which combines different data sources such as national accounts, survey data, fiscal data, and wealth rankings to produce its indices. In Figure 16, we observe the trajectory of the country's Gini index of wealth compared to the trajectory of the same index for Latin America from 1995 to 2021. According to WID data in 2017, the wealth Gini index for Chile was 0.911, more than double that of the *income* estimated by the Chilean Ministry of Social Development, the highest in Latin America, and 0.46 points higher than the regional Gini coefficient average for income.

The concentration of wealth of the richest 1 percent is also the highest in Latin America and one of the highest in the world, close to 50 percent of total wealth in 2021 (Figure 17). Arguably a high concentration of wealth from the

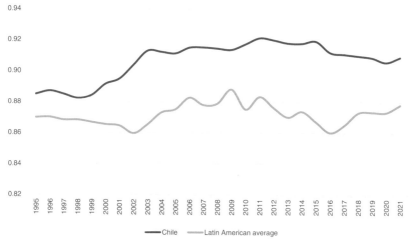

Figure 16 Gini index of wealth

Source: Own elaboration, data from WID (2022)

---

[50] Credit Suisse Research Institute (2019).

Figure 17 Top 1 percent net personal wealth share
Source: Graph provided by www.wid.world

elites might be a more severe issue than income inequality since wealth gets
passed on from one generation to the next (correcting for inheritance laws),
determining a person's economic position starting point in life and, very likely,
their lifetime position in society.

5.2.2 State's Redistributive Capacity

While in most OECD countries, there is a significant reduction in inequality
before and after the state's redistributive action, in Chile, we observe a very
reduced difference in both indices (inequality of income before and after state
taxes and transfers), suggesting little progressive redistribution of incomes (see
Figure 18). The data tend to show that in countries where redistribution significantly reduces market-driven inequality, most of the effort falls on the side of
state spending rather than taxes. In Chile, monetary transfers do not have
a significant redistributive impact, as they do in other OECD countries.
Before taxes and transfers, market-driven income inequality in Chile is like
that of Belgium and Austria and even lower than that of Finland, France, and
Ireland. However, after taxes and transfers, Chile's inequality is substantially
higher than in these countries.

The low redistributive capacity of the Chilean state has been identified as
a weakness that limits the impact of social spending (OECD, 2018b; World
Bank, 2017). Chile's public social spending, as a share of GDP, is low by

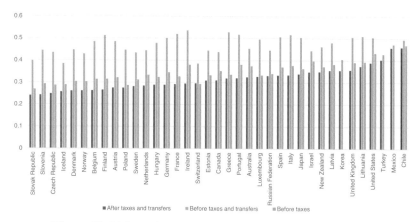

Figure 18 Gini Coefficient before and after taxes and transfers

Source: Own elaboration, data from OECD (2020)

international standards (see Figure 19a).[51] Total social spending represents 11.4 percent of the country's GDP, the second lowest among OECD countries and 8.6 percentage points below the OECD's average (OECD, 2022a). Although the public spending share on social programs has marginally increased since 2006, from 8.3 percent to 9.4 percent of GDP in 2019, it has not yet surpassed the share of 1987, when social spending represented 11.8 percent of GDP. Of course, the level of social spending is higher in absolute terms due to the much higher GDP in 2019 than in 1987 (see Figure 19b).

A low public spending-to-GDP ratio goes hand in hand with low tax revenue, equivalent to 19.3 percent of GDP in 2020, considerably lower than the OECD average of 33.5 percent, and the third lowest after that of Mexico and Colombia (Figure 20a).[52] Tax collection has increased only 2.4 percentage points since 1990 (Figure 20b).

While higher-income OECD countries collect taxes mainly from personal income and social security, Chile's tax revenue is concentrated in value-added tax (VAT) and corporate income tax.[53] Value-added tax is a regressive tax when measured as a share of current income. The tax burden as a share of income is highest for low-income households and falls sharply as household income rises since, in the wealthiest households, consumption represents a smaller fraction of income than in lower-income households. When including mandatory social

---

[51] Social expenditure comprises cash benefits, direct in-kind provision of goods and services, and tax breaks with social purposes.

[52] In Chile, most social contributions are paid into privately managed funds and are not included in the tax-to-GDP ratio.

[53] Tax on corporate profits is defined as taxes levied on the net profits (gross income minus allowable tax reliefs) of enterprises. It also covers taxes levied on the capital gains of enterprises.

Figure 19 Public social spending (A) and evolution of public spending (B)

Source: Own elaboration, data from OECD (2022a)

security contributions to private pension funds, Chile's tax revenue share is more similar to the OECD average, the main difference being that the personal income burden is much lower than in the rest of these countries (OECD, 2022b).

5.3 The Commodification of Public Social Services during the 1980s and Its Effect on the Provision of Social Goods and the Labor Market

5.3.1 Origins and Consequences of the Commodification of Public Social Services

Since the 2011 student protests demanding free, public, quality education in Chile, the discussion around the inequalities generated by the private provision of education and other social goods has become more frequent in the country.

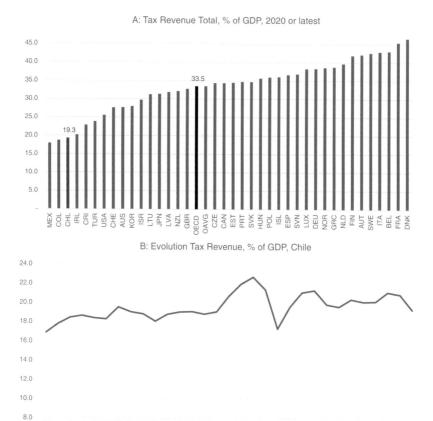

Figure 20 Tax revenue, percentage of GDP

Source: Own elaboration, data from OECD (2022a)

Later, there were mass social protests demanding higher pensions and the end of the privatized pension system – led by the No Más AFP movement – in 2016 and 2017 and the *estallido social* (social uprising) in October–November 2019. Several other demands were added, such as access to better public healthcare, cheaper public transport, and, of course, decent pensions.

The political response to all these social demands was channeled into writing a new constitution, which would replace the 1980 constitution approved during the military dictatorship. Among the criticisms of Pinochet's constitution was the *commodification of social services* – treating these services as a commodity traded in a market in which quality services could be acquired only by paying high prices to the detriment of the poor. The 1980 constitution stated a subsidiary role of the state in the provision of social goods, allowing only temporary participation of the public sector in areas in which the private sector could not do so due to technical limitations and/or because it was not profitable for them. Likewise, the state could not intervene in areas where individuals or groups in society were economically self-sufficient, favoring private solutions to social problems.

This doctrine has led to a reduction in the state's participation in economic and social life, while promoting private participation in critical spheres of daily life, such as healthcare, education, housing, and pensions. The involvement of the private sector in the provision of social goods has generated intense polarization and dual markets, in which recipients' ability to pay determines the quantity and quality of the service they could access.

On one hand, the public sector provides social services at a lower cost for users but generally the service could be in short supply (chronic excess demand as in the case of surgeries in public hospitals) and/or provision of lower quality. On the other hand, the private sector offers services of varying quality depending on users' capacity to pay.[54] Thus, people affiliated with the private health insurance system (Isapres), for example, have easier access to specialist appointments, surgeries, exams, and so on without being on the long waiting lists that affect the public healthcare system (Fondo Nacional de Salud [Fonasa]). The same occurs with education provision, in which the public sector is one of the many providers. Thus, a relatively weak state is expected to be responsible for the delivery of education and healthcare services to people with a limited budget or who cannot afford the private system. Incidentally, that segment can represent more than 80 percent of the population.

These differences in access to social services across different social segments, when combined with labor market dynamics, have the consequence of enhancing inequalities in other areas of life. For example, limited access to quality education for the poor translates into unequal opportunities in the labor market, which also influences wage-earning capacities, also placing limits on access to the healthcare system and reduced private contributions to the pension system. A vicious circle is set in motion. The rest of this section discusses the effects of the main privatizing policies in education, healthcare, pensions, and the labor market.

5.3.2 Education

The educational reform initiated in the 1980s handed public education over to the municipal administration and allowed the creation of private schools funded with state subsidies. Publicly funded education was delivered through a voucher system (a subsidy per student to each educational unit), which expanded access

---

[54] Sanhueza, Claudia; Telias, Amanda and Zapata-Román, Gabriela (2023). "Políticas sociales para un nuevo modelo de desarrollo en Economía, Ecología y Democracia: Hacia Un Nuevo Modelo De Desarrollo". Editors: Aldo Madariaga and Felipe Correa. Editorial Catalonia. ISBN: 9789564150079

to education, but at the same time contributed to increasing school segregation, giving schools greater freedom to choose the best students, rather than the original intent of letting students choose the best schools. In this way, the country fostered an educational system that reproduces initial inequalities faced by students regarding family background, income, housing, and neighborhood, rather than leveling up those inequalities. The privatized system has failed to improve the provision of education for less economically favored students, not only in quality, but also in the provision of educational infrastructure, access to new learning technologies, green areas, sports, and other extracurricular activities.

Even though public spending on primary and secondary education has increased and reforms have been introduced to reduce school segregation (particularly in Bachelet's second term in office, 2014–18), public education provision is rather limited. Only 35.5 percent of students go to public schools, while 55.3 percent attend privately managed schools that receive public funding (*colegios particulares subvencionados y de administración delegada*).[55] Only 9.2 percent of students go to purely private schools (*colegios particulares*). High participation of private actors in the educational system is not a problem per se if it provides a quality education that levels the playing field, particularly for vulnerable students. However, we observe significant disparity in quality and infrastructure since there are few incentives to invest in these issues versus increasing profits.

In practice, an equalization of education opportunities does not happen, and the quality of education each student receives is closely related to the socioeconomic status of their parents, limiting their possibilities of upward social mobility in the future. Thus 82 percent of students from a high socioeconomic status obtain good results on the standardized test (within the highest 25 percent of the distribution), and only 11 percent of low-income students get similar results (PNUD, 2017). Inequalities in the school system have long-term effects and determine the access to and performance in tertiary education and long-run earnings in the labor market.

Regarding higher education, although the percentage of people obtaining university and professional technical degrees in Chile has increased considerably in the past decade, from 15.7 to 25.8 percent of the population between twenty-five and sixty years old, there are still considerable differences in access and performance among people of different socioeconomic backgrounds (CASEN, 2006, 2017). Gaentzsch and Zapata-Román (2020) showed that exogenous circumstances at birth are highly correlated with educational outcomes. For instance, the probability of students with an Indigenous background completing higher education is five percentage points lower than that of a non-Indigenous person.

---

[55] The *corporaciones de administración delegada* are state-owned technical–vocational high schools representing 1.2 percent of secondary education enrollment. They are publicly funded and managed by private organizations linked to the business and industrial sectors.

This study also showed that other circumstances, such as parental background, influence students' educational achievement. In a context of equal opportunities, people with parents without formal education (or who did not complete primary education) would have the same chances of obtaining higher education as those with parents who did. In Chile, almost 10 percent of people with parents without formal education achieve a professional degree. However, this ratio is sixfold higher for people with parents who completed higher education.

These initial inequalities are also expressed in access to good jobs. Job opportunities are expected to level off once the student gets an academic degree. However, Gaentzsch and Zapata-Román (2020) observed that the average income of graduates with highly educated parents (also with university degrees) have more than twice the income of graduates whose parents did not complete primary education. Furthermore, the latter type of graduate obtains a similar average income to vocational (technical) education graduates but from families with higher educational achievement. This lends credibility to the argument that education is essential to secure a well-paid job, but other factors might be even more relevant. As inequality of opportunity theories suggest, parental education often intersects with other forms of advantage, such as financial and social capital.

The cost of higher education for students in Chile is very high. Tuition fees in public institutions in Chile are among the highest for a bachelor's program across countries with available data. National students were charged $8,317 per year, on average, for a bachelor's degree in 2019 (OECD, 2021). From the public expenditure, 35 percent of total educational spending (7.8 percent of GDP) goes to tertiary education; 61.1 percent of this expenditure is funded by students and their families primarily through student loans lent by private banks compared to a 31 percent equivalent average in the OECD (OECD, 2022c).

Before 2005, there was a differentiated funding system in which students from public (or traditional) universities (created before the reform in 1981) received loans from the state, and students from new private universities could only opt for personal bank loans. Banks determined which universities and careers received loans, according to potential future payment and availability of collateral, restricting this funding opportunity only to middle- and high-income groups. In 2005, the Crédito con aval del Estado (CAE) was created. All students could borrow their entire tuition fees without personal collateral since the state would act as a guarantor. Although this policy aimed to democratize access to higher education, it strongly increased enrollment in programs and universities of questionable quality, raising the indebtedness of the population under twenty-five.

Even though the CAE system is still in place, it is no longer the primary source of higher education funding. Since 2017, students from families in the lowest six income deciles have been exempt from tuition fees during the standard length of study. Undoubtedly this promises to be a step toward greater equality of opportunities for students from more disadvantaged sectors. However, the costs of higher education (tuition fees) remain among the highest of the OECD countries (OECD, 2021).

5.3.3 Health

The social reforms initiated during the military dictatorship also generated profound changes in the healthcare system. These included the creation of Fonasa, the municipalization of the primary healthcare system, the incorporation of a compulsory contribution of 4 percent of wages to healthcare, and the creation of Isapres, private companies that provide health insurance. They receive the mandatory workers' contributions that adhere to this system, which currently represent 7 percent of gross remuneration, providing healthcare benefits and the payment of medical working licenses.

As in education, incorporating private agents into the healthcare system has generated deep inequalities in access, quality of benefits, waiting times, and treatments. These translate into significant gaps in people's life expectancy related to their socioeconomic status. Research carried out by the Urban Health in Latin America (SALURBAL) project shows a gap of almost nine years for men and almost eighteen for women, with a peak in life expectancy in the highest-income counties of the capital Santiago.

In 2019, the public healthcare system covered almost 15 million people (77 percent of the population), of whom 53 percent are women (FONASA, 2019). The higher relative participation of women can be explained by the high cost of private insurance for women of reproductive age, almost double that for men of the same age group. On the other hand, nine out of ten people older than sixty use Fonasa, representing 27 percent of those affiliated with the system. Older adults also face higher costs and access restrictions in the private system.

Although public spending on healthcare has increased from 1.6 percent of GDP in 1990 to 4.7 percent in 2015, it is still below the average for OECD countries. While in OECD countries, 72 percent of healthcare spending is financed with public resources, in Chile, it is only 60 percent (World Bank, 2017). Below-average public spending translates into high private expenditure on health. In 2019, almost one-third of Chile's healthcare expenditures were paid directly by households, out-of-pocket payments that neither public nor private health insurance cover (World Bank, 2022d). This private spending on healthcare has increased in recent years, representing 6.3 percent of total household spending in 2015 ($55), which varies depending on family income, between $15 for the 20 percent with the lowest income and $132 for the richest 20 percent (World Bank, 2017).

One of the essential steps toward granting universal access to healthcare benefits was implementing the AUGE plan (Spanish acronym for Plan de Acceso Universal de Garantías Explícitas). The aim of AUGE (now called GES – Explicit Health Guarantees) was to guarantee coverage for a series of diseases considered a priority, regardless of whether people were subscribed to the public or private healthcare system. With the introduction of GES, a growing number of Isapres users migrated to the public system. Before the healthcare reform, there was already a growing discontent with private insurance institutions, which frequently refused treatment for preexisting illnesses and unilaterally increased the cost of healthcare coverage, charging differentiated prices according to the level of risk of the affiliates (prices for women of childbearing age and older adults).

In 2010, the state introduced stricter regulations to Isapres, suspending the mechanism of premiums adjusted by gender and age. However, an alternative mechanism was never proposed, so in practice, the cost of private health insurance still considers the risk of the affiliates as a central element, in which each person is responsible for their own risk. Despite the state regulating private providers, users must file individual lawsuits to avoid unilateral increases in their insurance and cancellation of contracts due to preexistence, instead of being protected by the regulator (Superintendencia de Isapres). In November 2022, the Supreme Court of Chile issued a ruling that forced the ISAPRES to restore excessive charges they made to their users since 2019 concerning differentiated risk premiums (by sex and age), equivalent to 1,400 million dollars. This threatens the survival of the private health insurance system, as we know it, in the country.

5.3.4 Pensions

The Chilean pension system, implemented in 1981, is a capitalization or individual savings system. It replaced a pay-as-you-go system with a system based on individual accounts in which compulsory pension savings funds are invested by for-profits pension fund management companies (AFP) that charge a fee (see Solimano 2021). The compulsory pension savings system contribution rate is 10 percent of the monthly salary of each worker. Initially, the new system promised pensions equivalent to 80 percent of the remuneration (replacement rate), but the reality after more than forty years of operation is average replacement rates of around 33–35 percent. In contrast, the rate of return earned by the AFP system was, between 2011 and 2021, 22.5 percent of the invested capital of the AFP. This promise, based on a high expected return on the funds and lower monthly contributions, made most active workers in the labor market switch in 1981 from the pay-as-you-go system to the new AFP system. New workers entering the labor market since that date joined the AFP system directly as they could not enter the publicly managed system that managed the pensions of those who remained in the old system.

The accumulated pension funds of wage earners in the hands of the AFP system (managed by six private firms) is $220 billion in 2019, equivalent to 70 percent of Chilean GDP. These funds, in turn, are the main source of low-cost capital for large Chilean corporations, commercial banks, and foreign corporations. Fund management companies charge a fee to every pension account and earn an average rate of return of 25–30 percent of the invested capital (Solimano, 2017, 2021). Most Latin American countries adopted this system in the 1990s along with many Eastern European countries, but since 2008, they, with the exception of Chile and Dominican Republic, have reverted to a mainly public system (Solimano, 2021, chapter 3).

Forty years after the start of the individual savings system, the pensions received by workers are much lower than the 80 percent of salary initially promised. In December 2020, the average monthly self-financed pension for workers was 264,831 Chilean pesos (approximately $270), and half of retired people got a pension of less than 154,654 Chilean pesos ($160). When adding the state pension contribution to very low self-funded pensions (Aporte Provisional Solidario [APS]), the average rises to 303,204 Chilean pesos ($310) and the median to 215,120 Chilean pesos ($220).

There is also a significant gender gap in pensions. When calculating the average pensions by gender, we observe that female pensions represent only 61 percent of males. That is, while men receive an average pension of 368,612 Chilean pesos ($380), women receive 227,621 Chilean pesos ($232) (self-financed plus APS), just above the individual poverty line of 170,821 Chilean pesos ($174) (as of December 2020). Thus, social protection is very limited in Chile since the pensions of many older adults are barely enough to survive.

From the creation of the AFP system until 2008, pensions paid depended exclusively on individual savings. In 2008, the state created the solidarity pension pillar, which aims to provide old-age (and disability) pensions to people of retirement age who have not had social security contributions, representing the poorest 60 percent of the population. Also, the solidarity pension complements the individual savings of the most vulnerable population. As of January 2021, the solidarity pension corresponds to 158,339 Chilean pesos ($161) for people aged between sixty-five and seventy-four and 169,649 Chilean pesos ($172) for people seventy-five years or older; both values are below the poverty line. This leads to almost 30 percent of older adults having to continue working, often in informal occupations (CIPEM, 2022).

An important step toward rising pensions, particularly for women and the middle class, is the creation of the Universal Guaranteed Pension (PGU), approved in early 2022. The PGU is a guaranteed pension paid by the state for people over sixty-five, equivalent to the poverty line, which only excludes the wealthiest 10 percent of the population. Another shortcoming of the privatized pension system is the channeling of pension mandatory savings of wage earners to finance investments of economic conglomerates (productive firms and banks) and the export of nearly one-third of the stock of pension savings abroad.

5.3.5 Labor Market

The Chilean labor market is characterized by low wages, high dependence on self-employment and short-term contracts, and high flexibility to unilaterally terminate contracts. As mentioned in the previous section, in 2018, 57 percent of employees, and 64 percent of female household heads, did not earn enough to lift an average family out of poverty.[56] Additionally, 51 percent of private-sector workers with full-time jobs were in the same situation, revealing high levels of precariousness in the job market.[57]

Other characteristics of the Chilean labor market include excessive dependence on self-employment and short-term contracts. Although it has decreased since 2012, the share of temporary contracts in Chile is the fourth highest among OECD countries – 27 percent – while the OECD average for this type of contract is 12 percent (OECD, 2022d). The level of informality, or the proportion of wage earners and self-employed workers not making contributions to the pension system, is also one of the highest in the OECD, standing at 32 percent of employment in 2015, held back only by cyclical conditions(OECD, 2018b).

Informality particularly affects lower-skilled workers, young people, immigrants, Indigenous people, and women. Temporary and informal workers generally face lower wages and frequent periods of unemployment and inactivity. Given that Chile has a private pension system based mainly on individual savings, high levels of informality put pressure on the pension scheme. For this reason, pension law established voluntary contributions for self-employed workers in 2014; these have only been compulsory since 2018 (SII, 2020).

Chilean labor market regulations may seem rigid de facto, but in practice, they are very pro-employer (or pro-capital), since it is quite easy for companies to hire and fire workers. The type of employment contract – permanent or temporary – is a fundamental distinguishing characteristic that creates a segmented or dual market, where temporary contracts are generally associated with flexibility and permanent contracts with rigidity (Ruiz-Tagle and Sehnbruch, 2015). Since 2011, there has been a downward trend in permanent contracts, which fell ten

---

[56] This is based on the monthly income poverty line for an average household of four people, which in November 2018 was 430,763 Chilean pesos ($621).

[57] Durán and Kremerman (2022).

percentage points to 65.7 percent in 2019. Most temporary hiring is found in large companies (more than 250 workers). While in micro-enterprises, 7.8 percent of employees have a temporary contract, in the case of large companies, this figure rises to 36.3 percent (ENCLA, 2019). While in more developed countries, a short-term contract can be the path to a permanent job, in Chile, only 4.1 percent lead to permanent jobs (ENCLA, 2019). Another factor that affects job stability is outsourcing; this is a common practice in Chile that in 2014 affected 17 percent of the workforce (ENCLA, 2014).

These practices limit employees' effective labor rights, preventing their access to severance pay, unions, and benefits such as nurseries. Other aspects of labor market flexibility include low unionization rates, limited strike rights (replacement of striking workers is allowed), decentralized and fragmented bargaining power, and highly flexible lay-off laws for workers on permanent contracts (OECD, 2018b).

The short duration of contracts and high job turnover also limits the coverage and benefits of unemployment insurance – which is financed with contributions from the employee and the employer. Only 50 percent of those whose contracts end in a year have enough contributions in their accounts to access unemployment insurance. In 2015, 50 percent of workers with a fixed-term contract had gaps in their contributions of more than three months, which prevents them from accessing the public unemployment fund (Fondo de Cesantía Solidario). All of this "flexibility" in the Chilean labor market transfers the risks from the employer (and the state) to the employee, leaving workers more vulnerable to external shocks and increasing inequality as there are no adequate safety nets (World Bank, 2017).

5.4 Conclusions

This section has analyzed the impact of social and economic reforms, of a neoliberal bent, that started during the dictatorship period (1973–90) and were largely maintained in the post-Pinochet restoration of democracy. Chile has made significant progress in reducing income poverty in the past two to three decades, but inequality of access to social services along with income and wealth inequality remain very high. Chile is still a country with significant differences in opportunities according to family, income, and racial back-grounds. The cost for the users of privately provided education and healthcare services is high and the level of pensions is low. According to the World Inequality Dataset, *wealth concentration* in Chile is the highest in Latin America, the most unequal region in the world.

The neoliberal reforms in their initial phase during the military dictatorship reduced fiscal capacity to reduce poverty and lower inequality and key functions of education, healthcare, and pensions were transferred to private providers.

Social assistance policies were targeted toward the poor and extremely poor populations abandoning universal policies. Social protection and unemployment benefits started being directly funded by workers, transferring macro and labor market risks to the workers in the formal sector, leaving those in the informal sector completely unprotected from external shocks and domestic downturns. With the return of democracy in 1990, more fiscal resources were devoted to social policy, but the general privatization of the delivery of social services was largely maintained. Over time and accelerating during the social protests of October 2019, citizen pressure for a welfare state and greater social rights has grown, which poses budgetary challenges for the state and resistance from the economic elites who do not want to pay higher taxes to finance social rights.

We must not lose sight of the fact that a sizable amount of the working population earns modest wages and experiences vulnerability to falling into poverty if there is a reversal of growth, inflation accelerates, and food prices increase. The much higher levels of multidimensional poverty than income poverty warn that income can be a restrictive yardstick to measure effective poverty and the satisfaction of basic needs by the population. Dissatisfaction with the neoliberal economic model and its features of low wages, expensive social services, and overall social inequality along with a style of governance that is perceived as detached from the aspirations of the rank and file of Chilean society exploded in the social protests of 2019.

6 Synthesis, Conclusions, and Challenges

In the three decades since the restoration of democracy, Chile has been portrayed as a successful case of economic development driven by free markets, macroeconomic sustainability, and reasonable political stability. The real picture, however, is more mixed, as we show in this Element. Progress and advancement are accompanied by social inequality, environmental fragility, and, at times, repressive politics (e.g., the Piñera government response to the uprising of October 2019). Chilean economic development must be analyzed in terms of its resource endowment of natural resources, chiefly mining products, forestry and fishery; its pattern of integration into the international economy; the legacies of colonial rule; and entrenched inequality with a powerful economic elite that manages to preserve its privileged role in the economy and society.

The constitutional history of Chile since independence is turbulent, with several constitutions in the first two decades of the nineteenth century followed by a centralistic and authoritarian constitution approved in 1833, a more progressive constitution in 1925, and another authoritarian constitution approved in 1980 oriented to protect the neoliberal economic model and preserve the institutional legacy of the Pinochet period. The rejection of a proposed constitution prepared by an elected convention with gender parity and Indigenous population participation on September 4, 2022, led to a second constitutional process, with narrow limits to proposed changes and entirely dominated by political parties and Congress.

Interestingly, the proposed constitutional chart presented in the plebiscite of September 4, 2022, was modern and innovative, including multinational representation of Indigenous populations, the assurance of social and economic rights, territorial decentralization, gender equality, and greater political and cultural diversity. However, a virulent campaign against its approval by right-wing sectors had an unexpected echo in the population that just two years before had voted to have a new constitution prepared by an independent constitutional convention and not by congress and/or the traditional political parties.

On the economic front, current features of the economy are inherited from the nineteenth and twentieth centuries. In the last third of the nineteenth century and up to the 1930s, Chile developed an economy dependent on valuable nitrate wealth obtained by the Chilean state, but run by British capital, after annexing the territories of the north following its victory in the war against Bolivia and Peru. This was complemented by good agricultural lands, an emerging services sector, and respectable industrial development.

In the nineteenth century, the country experienced a variety of monetary systems that included the adoption of bimetallism (gold and silver), free banking, cycles of currency convertibility and inconvertibility, the gold standard, and fiscal money. In the twentieth century, Chile created the Central Bank in 1925, but returned for a few years to the gold standard that was abandoned in 1931 at the time of the Great Depression. Between the 1940s and the 1970s (ISI strategy), the country suffered from chronic and at times explosive inflation and had a high dependence on exports of copper. It was vulnerable to terms-of-trade shocks and the availability of foreign lending. At the same time, it managed to build an industrial manufacturing and fostered the incorporation of the working class and the middle class to education, healthcare, pensions, housing and national politics in an increasingly participatory democracy.

The Central Bank followed during the ISI period various modalities of monetary and credit policy, including direct credits to the treasury and various government agencies. Chronic inflation was the norm and financial markets remained underdeveloped. In the neoliberal era, inflation was brought down at a large social cost and inequality sharply increased. In the 1990s, a new orthodoxy of independent central banking, inflation targeting, and fiscal rules replaced previous modalities of conducting monetary policy.

Chile's per capita income jumped from nearly $5,000 in the late 1980s to almost $29,000 in 2022 in purchasing power parity. However, this prosperity masks vast disparities in income levels across individuals and regions of the country. In turn, this prosperity has been, to an extent, borrowed, as it has relied on the intensive exploitation of nonreproducible natural resources, particularly since the 1990s. At the sector level, the economy has specialized in mining, finance, and services, with a diminished share of the manufacturing sector in output that reached a historical low of 10 percent of GDP in 2017.

The aggregate growth process of the past six decades has been volatile. Annual GDP growth was the highest in the 1990s and then it started to gradually decline along with productivity growth. In this period, two very big recessions occurred in 1975 (GDP contacted by 12 percent) and 1982–3 (the decline of GDP in the two years reached 16 percent), with more moderate recessions in 1999 and 2009. However, GDP contracted by more than 6 percent in 2020 in a COVID-led recession. Economic growth in the past two decades has been affected by slower productivity growth and the gradual loss of dynamism of the mining and services sectors. Along with stagnation trends, episodes of social unrest emerged, some very virulent, in a country of persistent inequalities and environmental fragility.

The patterns of ST show a decline in the value-added shares of manufacturing and agriculture and a rise in services, particularly finance, trade, hotels, and restaurants, with ups and downs in mining shares in the transition from the ISI strategy to the outward-orientated neoliberal model. These trends are more strongly accentuated for employment shares, with the decline in relative employment generation in agriculture and manufacturing going directly to the services sector, which currently accounts for two-thirds of total employment in the economy. Trade liberalization led to severe reductions in the value-added shares of textiles, metal-mechanic, and shoe factories within manufacturing.

The neoliberal revolution led by the Pinochet regime in the 1970s and 1980s brought about severe social costs, slow disinflation, and bubble-led growth. At the same time, it undertook capitalist modernization and opened the economy to international trade and capital mobility. In the 1990s, with the restoration of democracy, there was an overall continuity of the neoliberal economic model but somewhat tempered by higher social spending, more public investment, and some partial reforms in the social sectors.

Inequality has been a problem in Chilean society since Spanish rule, and this feature was not reversed after independence or throughout the nineteenth, twentieth, and early twenty-first centuries. Inequality declined in 1940–73, but increased sharply since the mid-1970s under the Pinochet regime; after the return of democracy, it has receded, although remaining at significant levels.

Social indicators for the past three decades display a mixed story: while total income-based poverty declined sharply from above 60 percent in the late 1980s to less than 10 percent in 2017 (new estimates), multidimensional poverty measured as gaps in access to education, healthcare, good jobs, and housing was nearly 20 percent in 2017 (the last year of official measurement). In turn, the Gini coefficient for total net wealth (around 90 percent, according to some estimates and near 70 percent according to others) is substantially higher than the net income Gini (nearly 50 percent), underscoring severe wealth inequality in Chile.

Student, environmental, women's and workers' organizations have been consistently critical of the neoliberal economic model and its features of low wages, expensive social services, territorial and social inequality, and over-exploitation of nonrenewable natural resources. The most severe break of social unrest, reaching very massive levels across the country, took place in October and November 2019. This is exacerbated by a style of governance by political elites perceived as largely detached from the aspirations of the rank and file of Chilean society.

Future trends in inequality and the prospect of more inclusive growth also remain uncertain. A Kuznets dynamic may be operating (in which at certain GDP per capita the economy becomes less unequal) as the gross and net income Gini coefficients have declined by five or six percentage points over the past fifteen to twenty years. The expansion of higher education from nearly 200,000 students to 1.3 million over this period has reduced the education premium and lessened labor income inequality, although this expansion of higher education has been accompanied by widespread student debt. In the future, the earnings capacities of low-income workers will depend on their access to quality public education at primary, secondary, and tertiary levels – a goal hampered by the current deterioration of public education at primary and secondary levels. Capital incomes, in turn, depend on interest earned on financial assets, dividend flows from physical assets, and profits from current production. Chile exhibits high levels of wealth inequality and household debt, which may be difficult to reduce through taxes on the very rich or other means because of political resistance to redistributive policies by powerful economic elites.

Chile faces several challenges to attaining a more balanced and sustainable development strategy consistent with the UNSDGs. A new productive structure is required to move away from the intensive use of natural resources – copper, sea resources, forestry, water – and toward knowledge-intensive sectors. A revival of the manufacturing sector must be complemented by clean production lines supported by a more environmentally conscious tax system. The reduction of high inequality and deconcentration of wealth requires political will and essential reforms in the tax system and the structure of markets, entailing effective antitrust legislation, deconcentration of ownership of the means of production, and the rebalancing of bargaining capacities between labor and capital to dampen the enormous economic surplus currently appropriated by wealthy elites. These reforms, if politically feasible, should enable more inclusive growth.

Finally, political uncertainties remain significant as the prospects for a new constitution that replaces the authoritarian constitution of 1980 are unclear after the defeat of the constitutional project in 2022 and the capture of the constitutional process by entrenched political elites, low-credibility political parties, and the congress. The rise of far right and populist, anti-immigration parties is another worrisome trend to monitor.

References

Alisjahbana, A. S., Sen, K., Sumner, A., and Yusuf, A. A. (2022), *The Developer's Dilemma: Structural Transformation, Inequality Dynamics, and Inclusive Growth*, Oxford University Press.

Alvarez, R. and Fuentes, J. R. (2006), "Trade Reforms and Manufacturing Industry in Chile," in Aroca, P. A. and Hewings, G. J. D. (eds.), *Structure and Structural Change in the Chilean Economy*, Palgrave Macmillan UK, pp. 71–94.

Banco Central. (2022), "Base de Datos Estadísticos," *Base de Datos Estadísticos*. https://goo.by/hjTFot (accessed November 25, 2022).

Barrientos, A. (2012), "Dilemas de las políticas sociales latinoamericanas. ¿Hacia una protección social fragmentada?" *Nueva Sociedad | Democracia y Política en América Latina*, May 1, vol. 239, pp. 65–78.

Bitar, S. (1979), *Transición, socialismo y democracia: La experiencia chilena*, Siglo Veintiuno Editores.

Blanchard, O., Dell'Ariccia, G., and Mauro, P. (2010), "Rethinking Macroeconomic Policy," *Journal of Money, Credit and Banking*, vol. 42, no. s1, pp. 199–215.

Comisión Económica para América Latina y el Caribe (CEPAL) y Organización de Cooperación y Desarrollo Económico (OCDE). (2005), *Evaluaciones del desempeño ambiental: Chile*, No. LC/L.2305, Comisión Económica para América Latina y el Caribe y Organización de Cooperación y Desarrollo Económico.

Conocimiento e Investigación en Personas Mayores (CIPEM). (2022), *Personas mayores y mercado del trabajo*, No. Empleo 2022, Conocimiento e Investigación en Personas Mayores.

Contreras, D. and Ffrench-Davis, R. (2012), "Policy Regimes, Inequality, Poverty and Growth: The Chilean Experience, 1973–2010," in Cornia, G. (ed.), *Falling Inequality in Latin America*, UNU-WIDER.

Corbo, V. and Solimano, A. (1991), "Chile's Experience with Stabilization Revisited," in Bruno, M., Fisher, S., Helpman, E., Liviatan, N., and Meridor, L. (eds.), *Lessons of Economic Stabilization and Its Aftermath*, MIT Press, pp. 57–101.

Corey, R. (2013), "The Hayek–Pinochet Connection: A Second Reply to My Critics." https://coreyrobin.com/2013/06/25/the-hayek-pinochet-connection-a-second-reply-to-my-critics (accessed November 28, 2022).

Cowan, K. N., Micco, A., Mizala, A., Pagés, C. P., and Romaguera, P. (2004), *Un diagnóstico del desempleo en Chile*, Inter-American Development Bank.

Credit Suisse Research Institute. (2019), *Global Wealth Report 2019*, Credit-suisse.com/researchinstitute.

Edwards, S. and Edwards, A. C. (1991), *Monetarism and Liberalization: The Chilean Experiment*, University of Chicago Press.

Encuesta de Caracterización Socioeconómica Nacional (CASEN). (2006), "Base de datos CASEN 2006," Ministerio de Desarrollo Social y Familia (Dataset).

Encuesta de Caracterización Socioeconómica Nacional (CASEN). (2017), "Base de datos CASEN 2017," Ministerio de Desarrollo Social y Familia (Dataset).

Encuesta Laboral (ENCLA). (2014), *Informe de resultados octava encuesta laboral*, Dirección del Trabajo. Ministerio del Trabajo y Previsión Social.

Encuesta Laboral (ENCLA). (2019), *Informe de resultados novena encuesta laboral*, Dirección del Trabajo. Ministerio del Trabajo y Previsión Social.

Fazio, H. (2005), *Mapa de la extrema riqueza al año 2005*, Lom Ediciones.

Fetter, F. W. (1931), *Monetary Inflation in Chile*, Princeton University Press.

Ffrench-Davis, R. (1973), *Políticas económicas en Chile 1950–70*, Ediciones Nueva Universidad.

Ffrench-Davis, R. (2002), *Economic Reforms in Chile: From Dictatorship to Democracy*, University of Michigan Press.

Ffrench-Davis, R. (2018), *Reformas económicas en Chile 1973–2017*, Penguin Random House Grupo Editorial Chile.

Fondo Nacional de Salud (FONASA). (2019), *Cuenta pública participativa*, FONASA.

Foxley, A. (1983), *Latin American Experiments in Neoconservative Economics*, University of California Press.

Gaentzsch, A. and Zapata-Román, G. (2020), "Climbing the Ladder: Determinants of Access to and Returns from Higher Education in Chile and Peru," *UNRISD Working Papers*, vol. 2020, no. 2.

Generadoras de Chile. (2022), "Generación eléctrica en Chile," *Generadoras de Chile*. http://generadoras.cl/generacion-electrica-en-chile (accessed November 25, 2022).

Grez Toso, S. (2009), "La ausencia de un poder constituyente democrático en la historia de Chile," *Revista iZQUIERDAS*, vol. año 3, no. 5.

Hayner, P. B. (2001), *Unspeakable Truths: Confronting State Terror and Atrocity*, Routledge.

Held, D. and Kaya, A. (2007), *Global Inequality: Patterns and Explanations*, Polity.

Herrendorf, B., Rogerson, R., and Valentinyi, Á. (2014), "Chapter 6: Growth and Structural Transformation," in Aghion, P. and Durlauf, S. N. (eds.), *Handbook of Economic Growth*, vol. 2, Elsevier, pp. 855–941.

Jadresic, E. (1986), *Evolución del empleo y desempleo en Chile, 1970–85*, no. 20, Corporación de Estudios para Latinoamérica (CIEPLAN).

Jorratt, M. (2009), *La tributación directa en Chile: Equidad y desafíos*, Comisión Económica para América Latina y el Caribe (CEPAL).

Kim, K. and Sumner, A. (2019), "The Five Varieties of Industrialisation: A New Typology of Diverse Empirical Experience in the Developing World," *ESRC GPID Research Network Working Paper*, no. 18.

Kornbluh, P. (2013), *Pinochet: Los archivos secretos*, Critica (Grijalbo Mondadori).

Durán, G. and Kremerman, M. (2022), "Los verdaderos sueldos de Chile: Panorama actual del valor de la fuerza de trabajo usando la Encuesta Suplementaria de Ingresos ESI (2021). http://doi.org/10.13140/RG.2.2.27736 .98563/1.

Larraín, F. and Meller, P. (1990), "La experiencia socialista–populista chilena: La Unidad Popular, 1970–73," *Cuadernos de Economía*, vol. 27, no. 82, pp. 317–355.

López, R., Figueroa, E., and Gutiérrez, P. (2013), "La 'Parte del León': Nuevas estimaciones de la participación de los super ricos en el ingreso de Chile," Working Papers 379, University of Chile, Department of Economics.

Lüders, R., Díaz, J., and Wagner, G. (2016), *La república en cifras: Historical statistics*, Ediciones UC.

McKinnon, R. I. (1973), *Money and Capital in Economic Development*, Brookings Institution Press.

McMillan, M. S. and Rodrik, D. (2011), *Globalization, Structural Change and Productivity Growth*, Working Paper No. 17143, National Bureau of Economic Research.

Meller, P. (1996), *Un siglo de economía política chilena (1890–1990): Un clásico de las ciencias sociales*, Uqbar Editores.

Ministerio de Desarrollo Social y Familia (MDSF). (2021), *CASEN 2020 en pandemia: Resumen de resultados pobreza por ingresos y distribución de ingresos*, Observatorio Social Ministerio de Desarrollo Social y Familia.

Ministerio de Desarrollo Social y Familia (MDSF). (2022), *Informe Final Panel de Expertos Para Mejoras al Instrumento de Focalización del Registro Social de Hogares*, Subsecretaría de Evaluación Social, Ministerio de Desarrollo Social y Familia, Chile.

Ministerio de Desarrollo Social y Familia (MDSF)and Programa de las Naciones Unidas para el Desarrollo (PNUD). (2020), *Evolución de la pobreza 1990– 2017: ¿Cómo ha cambiado Chile?* División del Observatorio Social de la Subsecretaría de Evaluación Social y el Programa de las Naciones Unidas para el Desarrollo, Chile.

Mkandawire, T. (2007), "Targeting and Universalism in Poverty Reduction," *Policy Matters: Economic and Social Policies to Sustain Equitable Development*, Zed Books, Third World Network, and United Nations.

Organisation for Economic Co-operation and Development (OECD). (2018a), "Income Distribution and Poverty: Overview." www.oecd.org/social/inequal ity.htm#income (accessed July 25, 2018).

Organisation for Economic Co-operation and Development (OECD). (2018b), *OECD Economic Surveys: Chile*, Overview, Organisation for Economic Co-operation and Development.

Organisation for Economic Co-operation and Development (OECD). (2020), *Tax Policy Reforms 2020: OECD and Selected Partner Economies*, Organisation for Economic Co-operation and Development.

Organisation for Economic Co-operation and Development (OECD). (2021), *Education at a Glance 2021: OECD Indicators*, Organisation for Economic Co-operation and Development. http://doi/org/10.1787/b35a14e5-en.

Organisation for Economic Co-operation and Development (OECD). (2022a), "Social Protection – Tax Revenue – OECD Data," *OECD Data*. http://data .oecd.org/socialexp/social-spending.htm (accessed October 18, 2022).

Organisation for Economic Co-operation and Development (OECD). (2022b), *OECD Economic Surveys: Chile 2022*. Organisation for Economic Co-operation and Development.

Organisation for Economic Co-operation and Development (OECD). (2022c), "Education Resources – Education Spending – OECD Data," *OECD Data*. http://data.oecd.org/eduresource/education-spending.htm (accessed October 24, 2022).

Organisation for Economic Co-operation and Development (OECD). (2022d), "Employment – Temporary Employment – OECD Data," *OECD Data*. http://data.oecd.org/emp/temporary-employment.htm (accessed October 24, 2022).

Organisation for Economic Co-operation and Development (OECD) and United Nations (UN) (2018), *Production Transformation Policy Review of Chile: Reaping the Benefits of New Frontiers*, Organisation for Economic Co-operation and Development.

Palma, J. G. (2022), "Latinoamérica es la región con el menor crecimiento de la productividad en el mundo desde las reformas neoliberales. La nueva trampa del ingreso medio: Rentas fáciles no generan precisamente élites schumpe-terianas," *El Trimestre Económico*, vol. 89, no. 355, pp. 943–977.

Programa de las Naciones Unidas Para el Desarrollo (PNUD). (2017), *Desiguales: Orígenes, cambios y desafíos de la brecha social en Chile*, Programa de las Naciones Unidas Para el Desarrollo.

Ramírez Necochea, H. (1958), "Balmaceda y la contrarrevolución de 1891," *Santiago*: *Editorial Universitaria*.

Rodriguez Weber, J. E. (2014), La economía política de la desigualdad de ingreso en Chile: 1850–2009, Tesis Doctorado, Universidad de la República (Uruguay). Facultad de Ciencias Sociales, Uruguay.

Rodrik, D. (2016), "Premature Deindustrialization," *Journal of Economic Growth*, vol. 21, no. 1, pp. 1–33.

Rosas, P. R. and Benítez, J. (2009), *La república inconclusa: Una nueva constitución para el bicentenario*, Editorial ARCIS.

Ruiz-Tagle, J. and Sehnbruch, K. (2015), "More but Not Better Jobs in Chile? The Fundamental Importance of Open-Ended Contracts," *International Labour Review*, vol. 154, no. 2, pp. 227–252.

Salazar, G. (2009), *Del poder constituyente de asalariados e intelectuales: (Chile, siglos XX y XXI)*, LOM Ediciones.

Servicio de Impuestos Internos (SII). (2020), "Cotizaciones previsionales obligatorias para trabajadores independientes," *Servicio de Impuestos Internos*. www.sii.cl/portales/renta/2016/cotizacion_previsional.htm.

Shaw, E. S. (1973), *Financial Deepening in Economic Development*, Oxford University Press.

Simoes, A. J. G. and Hidalgo, C. A. (2011), "The Economic Complexity Observatory: An Analytical Tool for Understanding the Dynamics of Economic Development," *Workshops at the Twenty-Fifth AAAI Conference on Artificial Intelligence*.

Sociedad Nacional de Mineria (SONAMI). (2019), *Estadisticas de precios*, Sociedad Nacional de Mineria.

Solimano, A. (1993), "Chile," in Taylor, L. (ed.), *The Rocky Road to Reform: Adjustment, Income Distribution, and Growth in the Developing World*, MIT Press.

Solimano, A. (1999), "The Chilean Economy in the 1990s: On a Golden Age and Beyond," in Taylor, L. (ed.), *After Neoliberalism: What Next for Latin America?* University of Michigan Press.

Solimano, A. (2010), *International Migration in the Age of Crisis and Globalization: Historical and Recent Experiences*, Cambridge University Press.

Solimano, A. (2012a), *Chile and the Neoliberal Trap: The Post-Pinochet Era*, Cambridge University Press.

Solimano, A. (2012b), *Capitalismo a la chilena: Y la prosperidad de las elites*, Editorial Catalonia.

Solimano, A. (2016), *Global Capitalism in Disarray: Inequality, Debt, and Austerity*, Oxford University Press.

Solimano, A. (2017), *Pensiones a la chilena*, Editorial Catalonia.

Solimano, A. (2020), *A History of Big Recessions in the Long Twentieth Century*, Cambridge University Press.

Solimano, A. (2021), *The Rise and Fall of the Privatized Pension System in Chile: An International Perspective*, Anthem Press.

Solimano, A. (2022), *Economic and Political Democracy in Complex Times: History, Analysis and Policy*, Taylor & Francis.

Solimano, A., Aninat, E., and Birdsall, N. (2000), *Distributive Justice and Economic Development: The Case of Chile and Developing Countries*, University of Michigan Press.

Solimano, A. and Gutierrez, M. (2008), "Savings, Investment and Capital Accumulation," in Dutt, A. K. and Ros, J. (eds.), *International Handbook of Development Economics. Vol. 1*, Edward Elgar, pp. 269–289.

Solimano, A. and Pollack, M. (2007), *La mesa coja: Prosperidad y desigualdad en el Chile democrático*, Centro Internacional de Globalización y Desarrollo, CIGLOB.

Solimano, A. and Zapata-Román, G. (2022), "Structural Transformations and the Lack of Inclusive Growth: The Case of Chile," *The Developer's Dilemma: Structural Transformation, Inequality Dynamics, and Inclusive Growth*, Oxford University Press, pp. 227–253.

Solow, R. M. (1956), "A Contribution to the Theory of Economic Growth,"*Quarterly Journal of Economics*, vol. 70, no. 1, pp. 65–94.

Subercaseaux, G. (1922), *Monetary and Banking Policy of Chile*, Clarendon.

Sumner, A. (2017), "The Developer's Dilemma: The Inequality Dynamics of Structural Transformations and Inclusive Growth," *ESRC GPID Research Network Working Paper*, Vol. 1.

Sunkel, O. (1994), "La crisis social de América Latina: Una perspectiva neoestructuralista," in Contreras, C. and Comisión Sudamericana de Paz, Seguridad y Democracia (eds.), *El desarrollo social: Tarea de todos*, Nueva Sociedad, pp. 13–44.

Sunkel, O. and Cariola, C. (1982), *Un siglo de historia economica de Chile, 1830–1930: Dos ensayos y una bibliografia*, Ediciones de Cultura Hispanica.

Vuskovic, P. (1993), "Obras escogidas sobre Chile 1964–1992," in Maldonado, R. (ed.), *Colección chile en el siglo XX*, Ediciones Centro de Estudios Políticos Latinoamericanos Simón Bolívar.

World Bank. (2017), *La república de Chile diagnóstico sistemático de país: La evolución hacia una sociedad más próspera*, No. 107903–CL, World Bank.

World Bank. (2020), "Gini Index (World Bank Estimate): Chile," *Data Bank Microdata Catalog.* https://data.worldbank.org/indicator/SI.POV.GINI?locations=CL (accessed November 10, 2020).

World Bank. (2022a), "DataBank Microdata Data Catalog: Chile." https://data.worldbank.org/country/chile (accessed November 8, 2021).

World Bank. (2022b), *Charting a Course towards Universal Social Protection: Resilience, Equity, and Opportunity for All*, World Bank.

World Bank. (2022c), "Tax Revenue (% of GDP): Chile | Data." https://data.worldbank.org/indicator/GC.TAX.TOTL.GD.ZS?locations=CL (accessed November 7, 2022).

World Bank. (2022d), "Out-of-Pocket Expenditure (% of Current Health Expenditure): Chile | Data," *Data Bank Microdata Catalog*. https://data.worldbank.org/indicator/SH.XPD.OOPC.CH.ZS?locations=CL (accessed October 22, 2022).

World Inequity Database (WID). (2022), "Chile," *WID: World Inequality Database*. https://wid.world/country/chile (accessed November 8, 2020).

About the Authors

Andrés Solimano holds a PhD in economics from the Massachusetts Institute of Technology. He is founder and chairman of the International Center for Globalization and Development, chairman of the Chilean chapter of the 1818 Society, chair of the governance board of the Investment Migration Council, and a board member of the Chilean Watercolor Foundation (Casa de la Aquarela). Dr. Solimano served as the country director at the World Bank, the executive director at the Inter-American Development Bank, the director of the Chile office of the Latin American School of Social Sciences, and the director of a project on the international mobility of talent with the United Nations University–World Institute of Economic Research in Helsinki. Dr. Solimano is frequently invited to deliver guest lectures at main universities and public forums globally, and he holds two regular programs on Chilean radio.

His most recent books as sole author include *Economic Democracy and Political Democracy* (Routledge, 2022),*The Evolution of Contemporary Arts Markets* (Routledge, 2021), *The Rise and Fall of the Privatized Pension System in Chile* (Anthem Press, 2021), *A History of Big Recessions in the Long 20th Century* (Cambridge University Press, 2020), *Global Capitalism in Disarray, Inequality, Debt, and Austerity* (Oxford University Press, 2017), *Pensiones a la Chilena* (Editorial Catalonia, 2017), *Economic Elites, Crises and Democracy* (Oxford University Press, 2014), *International Migration in the Age of Crisis and Globalization* (Cambridge University Pres, 2010), and other volumes. He is also the editor of *The International Mobility of Talent: Types, Causes and Development Impact* (Oxford University Press, 2008).

Gabriela Zapata Román is an economist with a PhD in development policy from the University of Manchester, United Kingdom. She is a researcher at the Max Planck–UCEN Research Group on the Economy and Society of the Faculty of Economics, Government and Communications at the Universidad Central de Chile, and an honorary research fellow at the Global Development Institute of the University of Manchester. Previously she has been a consultant for the German Institute of Development and Sustainability, the World Bank, the United Nations Research Institute for Social Development, and the United Nations University World Institute for Development Economics Research. Her research interests include the topics of structural transformations and inclusive growth, gender and labor inequalities, inequality of opportunities, and intergenerational mobility. The author acknowledges the support of the Chilean Research and Development Agency, Fondecyt Postdoctorado No. 3210480.

Cambridge Elements ☰

Development Economics

Rachel M. Gisselquist
UNU-WIDER

Rachel M. Gisselquist is a Senior Research Fellow and member of the Senior Management Team of UNU-WIDER. She specializes in the comparative politics of developing countries, with particular attention to issues of inequality, ethnic and identity politics, foreign aid and state building, democracy and governance, and sub-Saharan African politics. Dr Gisselquist has edited a dozen collections in these areas, and her articles are published in a range of leading journals.

Shareen Joshi
Georgetown University

Shareen Joshi is an Associate Professor of International Development at Georgetown University's School of Foreign Service in the United States. Her research focuses on issues of inequality, human capital investment and grassroots collective action in South Asia. Her work has been published in the fields of development economics, population studies, environmental studies and gender studies.

Patricia Justino
UNU-WIDER and IDS – UK

Patricia Justino is a Senior Research Fellow at UNU-WIDER and Professorial Fellow at the Institute of Development Studies (IDS) (on leave). Her research focuses on the relationship between political violence, governance and development outcomes. She has published widely in the fields of development economics and political economy and is the co-founder and co-director of the Households in Conflict Network (HiCN).

Marinella Leone
University of Pavia

Marinella Leone is an assistant professor at the Department of Economics and Management,University of Pavia, Italy. She is an applied development economist. Her more recent research focuses on the study of early child development parenting programmes, on education,and gender-based violence. In previous research she investigated the short-, long-term and intergenerational impact of conflicts on health, education and domestic violence.She has published in top journals in economics and development economics.

Jukka Pirttilä
University of Helsinki and UNU-WIDER

Jukka Pirttilä is Professor of Public Economics at the University of Helsinki and VATT Institute for Economic Research. He is also a Non-Resident Senior Research Fellow at UNU-WIDER. His research focuses on tax policy, especially for developing countries. He is a co-principal investigator at the Finnish Centre of Excellence in Tax Systems Research.

Andy Sumner
King's College London, and UNU-WIDER

Andy Sumner is Professor of International Development at King's College London; a Non-Resident Senior Fellow at UNU-WIDER and a Fellow of the Academy of Social Sciences. He has published extensively in the areas of poverty, inequality, and economic development.

About the Series

Cambridge Elements in Development Economics is led by UNU-WIDER in partnership with Cambridge University Press. The series publishes authoritative studies on important topics in the field covering both micro and macro aspects of development economics.

United Nations University World Institute for Development Economics Research

United Nations University World Institute for Development Economics Research (UNU-WIDER) provides economic analysis and policy advice aiming to promote sustainable and equitable development for all. The institute began operations in 1985 in Helsinki, Finland, as the first research centre of the United Nations University. Today, it is one of the world's leading development economics think tanks, working closely with a vast network of academic researchers and policy makers, mostly based in the Global South.

Cambridge Elements ≡

Development Economics

Elements in the Series

The 1918–20 Influenza Pandemic: A Retrospective in the Time of COVID-19
Prema-chandra Athukorala and Chaturica Athukorala

Parental Investments and Children's Human Capital in Low-to-Middle-Income Countries
Jere R. Behrman

Great Gatsby and the Global South: Intergenerational Mobility, Income Inequality, and Development
Diding Sakri, Andy Sumner and Arief Anshory Yusuf

Varieties of Structural Transformation: Patterns, Determinants, and Consequences
Kunal Sen

Economic Transformation and Income Distribution in China over Three Decades
Cai Meng, Bjorn Gustafsson and John Knight

Chilean Economic Development under Neoliberalism: Structural Transformation, High Inequality and Environmental Fragility
Andrés Solimano and Gabriela Zapata-Román

A full series listing is available at: www.cambridge.org/CEDE

Printed in the United States
by Baker & Taylor Publisher Services